KILTY-BOY

KILTY-BOY

Kevin Barry

authorHOUSE®

AuthorHouse™
1663 Liberty Drive
Bloomington, IN 47403
www.authorhouse.com
Phone: 1-800-839-8640

First published by AuthorHouse   07/07//2011

ISBN: 978-1-4567-8462-1 (sc)
ISBN: 978-14567-8461-4 (ebk)

Printed in the United States of America

Chapter One

'Shall I start at the end and go back to the beginning? Or shall I go back to the beginning and start at the end? While you are making that one out, I'll make a start.' Uncle Jack in a few short sentences had tied me up, unaccountably, all in knots.

'Sure, it is a strange world that we are living in,' my Ma would always quip. For me, she was the greatest quipper in the world bar none.

'Things are sent to try us. They surely are. Well, they are.' Uncle Paddy emphasises the fact. 'Life is a conundrum.' He pauses. 'I would agree with that, if I had the faintest idea what conundrum meant in the first place!'

I'll be welcoming you to my world in order that you will not the blazes be left in the dark. It is now the late 1950s in Notting Hill.

'No surrender!' Uncle Paddy is living in some kind of a time - warp. After a few jars he loses all else of proportion, time, and place. It is a boozy location he falls into, a kind of convenient comfort zone. Especially at this time of the day, life becomes a bit of a blur. 'No surrender!' echoes down through the ancient streets and byways and still exists in the wee small hours of the awakening morning. Semblances of an era have somehow shifted and passed away before his weakening eyes.

It is a time for introductions, a breaking of the ice so to speak. I like to think of it as an aspect of hospitality being warmed up. Nonetheless, it can be described as an eternal enigma or, alternatively, something that has a sense of extreme importance.

In the meantime, I'll put the kettle on as I dust the cobwebs off from my brain and wish you a hearty top of the morning. Kevin is my name, the fifth and final child to Carthage and Margaret Barry.

It's as strange as strange can be, but when I reached the grand old age of seven I felt I was beginning to be a very self-aware 'garcoon', i.e.,

1

a young boy as my Irish relatives are apt to refer to myself. Some of my very first recollections were standing on the outside steps of the first and second floor flat in the ever open front door of 98 St Stephen's Gardens, West London. I watched the world pass me by with saucer-shaped and wondrous eyes.

My mother was always on my case to pray. She for her part was forever praying at home or in the church. I did try my best to be a good lad, but vital questions such as 'When is the soccer being played?', 'What's on at the local cinema?', and (not to forget) 'Are we having fish and chips this particular evening?' all somehow managed to get in the way. But I did, nevertheless, thank Him once in a while for all kinds of things that He had done for me, including my family, my friends, and my life in general—and also for Miss Hathaway, my form teacher in my infants' school. She was always so cool and looked and smelled of roses. And most importantly of all, she was always kind and loving to me

I went to school in Latymer Road, which was about a mile away from the 'Gardens.' The school was a very old place. Miss Hathaway informed all us students that it dated from the Victorian period. Also, she encouraged all of us that if there was anything that we wanted to know, she would be more than happy to help us.

I put my hand up, and she asked me what was my question was. I asked her, 'Miss, why is life so dead serious?' I don't think she heard me properly, because she didn't seem to answer but smiled broadly and asked the other pupils if there was anything else that they wanted to ask her. I must admit now that I have always found grown - ups rather odd at times.

I didn't mind going to school, but I was always glad when the bell rang at 4.00 p.m. for me to depart for home. At school I sometimes felt when I was there—well, how can I explain it?—a wee bit shut up. Me, I prefer to be free outside of its confining walls. Shortly after 4.00 p.m., my sister Eileen turned up and duly rescued me. She herself attended a girls' school close by.

I had a very embarrassing incident there on one occasion. It concerned a little hill in my school playground that I had a tendency to sit upon. The problem was that this hill had little stones in it, and they caused the seat of my pants to split open when I sat on it. All of the other children made fun of me when they saw my torn and ragged bottom. Some clever Charlie in my class tried to be smart when he jokingly said to me, 'Hey there, Kevin, why are you wearing "holy pants"?'

I didn't reply and pretended I didn't hear him because I didn't think that remark was very funny.

My mum says that many people should not look so miserable and they should not have faces like 'a long wet weekend.' Her solution for beating the blues was to drink gallons of tea and lots of milk with heaps of sugar. She proclaimed, 'It's the sweet "tae" and the praying that keeps me going.'

I am so thrilled that I had learned to read early on in my life. The result can be that the world can become a much more exciting and interesting to be in. I nearly forgot to mention that at this stage of my life I'd just finished reading the short novel *The Little Prince*. It was a great read. I definitely considered him to be a lad after my own heart. Did you know that he was from a small and distant planet? How 'cosmic' was that for starters? My grandpa told me he thought I am was from another planet too.

At this time, I discovered the wonderful world of butterflies. Miss Hathaway loved them as well and said that they were one of the miracles of nature. It was truly wonderful to see them in their evolving state where they look to be in a tremendous struggle. Aye, for sure, they certainly looked all crimply, hot and bothered, and at this stage well and truly up against it. However, against all the odds, they came out of their restricting cocoon all beautiful and triumphant as they fly off into the open sky dressed in their resplendent colours.

Living in Notting Hill in the late 1950s was not all fun. Not at all. Where we lived it was so overcrowded you really wouldn't believe it. A family of six lived in the basement. A family of seven inhabited the ground floor. There were seven of my own clan on the first and second floors. And a family of five lived on the third floor. It was incredibly difficult facing up and coming to terms with all the 'pongy' smells that emanated from this dwelling, what with all the babies and the nappies and an endless queue for each of the two loos, not to mention the frequent visits from a few of the inhabitants and customers of the local pubs. Need I say any more? My visiting Grandma said that our place was not for the squeamish!

The situation wasn't helped by the fact that the landlord refused to replace our rusty old bath in the 'bathroom boutique' as my friend Helen called it. This was situated between the first and second landing of our dwelling. Consequently, yours truly had to bathe in his 'birthday suit' right in front of the fireplace in our living room. Not funny.

This room was situated on the second floor. It had a rather worn out three-piece suite (more so because I liked to rock continually to and fro on the settee and on the two armchairs), an antique dining table, a dressing table that had seen better days, and an 'open plan' kitchen. Next to it was my bedroom, which I shared with my brother who is the eldest in our family. It wasn't a very big room, but our double bed fitted in nicely with a small wardrobe. My brother tied a string around the switch of the light and angled the string to the end of our bed. When it was time to turn the light at night, we didn't have to get up from our bed but just pulled the string. He was smart, my brother Michael.

There were two other bedrooms on the first floor. My parents had one of the rooms. Their room was simple and sparsely furnished, similar to what my brother and myself had. However, my three sisters shared the other bedroom, which was our poshest room by far, with its nice quilts, cushions, and a fancy dressing-table.

One thing that I was very grateful for and what made life worthwhile around our area was the recreational area situated at the back of our dwelling. Funnily enough, it was called the 'Back.' It was about a hundred yards long and twenty yards wide. There were some swings at one end, and about a third of the area was turf. The other two thirds was a concrete area which my friends and I would use as a soccer pitch in summer and cricket venue in the summer. I loved the Back—a wonderland. It was my very own playground, a kind of extension of my little world where I would dream of soccer and of every possible kind of sporting glory.

My brother came up with another bright idea when he suggested that the whole family club together to get a television set on the hire purchase. My parents didn't have very much money to afford a TV set, so this was a welcome solution. We were one of the first families around our area to get a TV installed. For a few short weeks, we were like celebrities in our neighbourhood as we let curious folk in for a glimpse at our own 'mini-Hollywood'. This turned out to be a super-duper idea! You know, it's a fact—there's nothing like a bit of popularity. And what made it even better was that Ma made sure I didn't have to give anything towards its cost when she announced that I hadn't 'a splink'. I think she meant to say I hadn't too much sense as yet, but I was sure I had!

Michael was now fourteen, Eileen was thirteen, Rita was eleven, and Maureen was nine years of age. I was the youngest child and Mum's 'pet.' And do you know what? I didn't mind a bit. Not me. Let's be honest, there's nothing wrong with a bit of mollycoddling now and again.

My parents met at a very famous place in London. It was at Speaker's Corner in Marble Arch. It is opposite Oxford Street in the West End. Grandpa says it is a great place to meet, because there is nothing more important than having free speech. He revealed that many people in the world do not have this basic human right, and people who do should be eternally grateful for it. I thought to myself that this was a very fair point to make

I loved being five years. I adored being six. But when I got to be seven, it was a year I surely would not forget in a hurry. My Uncle Paddy informed me that grownups had a word for it. It was called: m-o-m-e-n-t-o-u-s. Phew! What a word! I can hardly bring myself to say it even now. Notwithstanding, it was a 'quare' and an odd thing that Uncle Paddy himself was the chief and main cause of myself being given the nickname of 'Kilty-boy.' I'll tell you all about it later. And I will also fill you in on the annual Irish Folk Festival held at the Porchester Hall. The latter was a large meeting place that was situated not too far from my family home in a place named Westbourne Grove.

I attended my one and only Irish dance lesson as a green youngster. I was quite enthusiastic about going there because I loved dancing and I just adored listening to music. Unfortunately, the dance teacher, Mrs O 'Riordan, didn't have much admiration for my dancing ability, and what is more she told me so in no uncertain way. What made it even worse, she declared in front of all the other dance students that I had two left feet and that I should stick to playing football instead. Now, to be truthful, these remarks didn't do too much for my confidence. 'What a bummer!' I thought. I would now have to aspire to another profession. And thus ended my brief dancing career, or so I thought at the time.

I have always loved fancy dress, even from an early age. My favourite costumes of all time were being a pirate, a cowboy, an Indian, and, of course, getting togged out into my special spaceman suit. 'Cosmic' is a word my eldest sister Eileen was always saying. Yes, I could see myself being a cool, cool astronaut.

My first girlfriend was named Carol. She lived in the basement next door to me. She was very good-looking. I heard once some other boy admirer reveal that she had a complexion like peaches and cream. Yes, she was beautiful. Carol always dressed so trendy like a junior film star. I am telling you no word of a lie. Yet when Pa saw me playing doctors and nurses with her one night, he was far from amused. He proclaimed under his breath that I resembled 'a right and proper eejit', (This is somebody who is a bit of a twit! I know he didn't really mean it though.) He continued to inform me with a red face that I could be mistaken for an Egyptian mummy with all the white sheets that I had wrapped around myself. Not knowing what he was referring to, I replied, 'Did the Egyptian mummy get on with her Egyptian daddy?' He just ignored me.

I have always found churches such wonderful and peaceful locations. I made my first communion at St Francis of Assisi near my school in Latymer Road when I was seven. All the family were there to see me. They were all so proud. Ma gave me two shillings and sixpence to spend. I loved her more than ever then. The altar looked so splendid and shiny with the gold and silver all around. It was great how the lights lit up the stained-glass windows.

I sometimes used to go shopping with Ma on Saturday afternoon in the Portobello Road. This was a 'groovy' and a busy market where you could buy just about anything you could think of. However, Ma mainly stuck to just buying her groceries there. However, I didn't see too much of Pa as he was always working long hours as a scrap-metal worker. Ma for her part was a cleaning woman. My father liked to go to the pub now and then as many Irish men have always done. He worked hard week in and week out, so in my opinion he deserved a pint or two. Nonetheless, of much more consequence, Ma loved Pa, and in turn, Pa loved Ma, and they both loved their five children. I knew this because Margaret told me so and informed us also that Carthage was of the same mind as her, but sometimes my father was somewhat a bit shy and a little slow in coming forward. I loved Pa.

On Sunday my whole family and I would go to St Mary of the Angels, our local church in nearby Moorehouse Road. We usually attended either at 10.00 a.m. or the 11.00 a.m., service. My mother went to church every single day of the week and prayed for everyone she knew. And she prayed for me, too, because she told me so.

It was great to light a candle now and again when I went to church. Margaret would always give me a few coppers to purchase the candle. Then I would light it and proceed to offer up my prayer. I usually liked to see the candle burn for quite a while in order to feel I was getting my money's worth. Yet if I was with my brother or either of my sisters, they would often say that I had to leave early with them because they hadn't got all day to be gazing at a candle. It was a shame really, I felt, as everyone seemed to be in such a rush in these times.

There was once a Catholic procession that wound its way through the Gardens. I think it was called 'Queen of the May'. As far as I was aware, it was an act of devotion to the Virgin Mary. Most Catholics I knew seemed to like the Virgin Mary. I didn't take part in the procession, as I felt that I wasn't too keen on marching. Nevertheless, it's a matter of choice, and each to his own.

Well, as 'the flock' were approaching, I was playing 'penny up the wall' with my new friend Johnny Hastings. When Ma got wind of what I was doing, she told me in no uncertain terms to stop immediately and to come inside to our place in order to show some respect for this religious event. When I arrived inside, she proclaimed, 'You'd shame a nation.' This was something she would say to me occasionally, but I always knew she never really meant it.

One thing that I loved about Saturday morning was the 'Saturday Morning Cinema' which was located at the Odeon in Westbourne Grove, West London. I loved this special feature especially for us kids. Cartoons were great. Westerns were right on. And the main feature-length film was the tops. There was also a serial which has a cliffhanging ending that left us young'uns hanging on the edge of our seats. Brilliant! Other things that made me happy were the lollies, ice cream, and sweets that I could buy there. My sister Maureen would take me to 'the pictures', as Margaret thought that if I was left to myself, I might get lost in the Odeon and might never find my way home ever again.

Another hobby I liked to follow was swimming. I was able to do this at the Porchester Hall. I loved swimming, although to be honest I was never much of a swimmer but—how should I put it?—more of a floater. I loved my own version of the backstroke that consisted of making as few strokes as possible whilst keeping afloat and looking up at the sky as the world went by. I spent hours and hours of great fun splashing around in my own 'Atlantic'. I would try my hand at practising a lot of the other swimming strokes as well as the crawl, the breast stroke, and the butterfly. However, as hard as I would try with my constant efforts to swim, I always seemed to inevitably slip gradually to the bottom of the pool.

On one occasion, I just survived Eileen's vigorous attempts to practice her 'life-saving' skills on me at the pool. She actually dragged me out of the boy's showers in order to do so. Talk about flamin' enthusiasm! And to make matters even worse, later on in the afternoon, she even left me in the arms of a friendly Indian man. He was supposed to be a survival expert! After half an hour of yours truly thrashing around like a fish pulled out the deep blue sea, he eventually released me. Just as well, as I thought I was on the verge of drowning.

Mind you, although it was fun and games most of the time at the baths, it was not always plain sailing. Believe it or not, on one occasion some 'clever Herbert' arrived and snatched all of my clothes from the changing room. If Eileen hadn't arrived with some replacement gear, I might have had to return home naked apart from a skimpy pair of swimming trunks.

Another hobby that I have already mentioned to you is football, 'the beautiful game'. I played everywhere. Apart from the Back, there were the streets and the school playground. There was Regent's Park and also Buck Hill, which was at the top end of Kensington Gardens and was another great spot. Buck Hill—I loved it, with its fresher air and wide-open green spaces. It was my little piece of country heaven inside the crowded city. It was brilliant there. It is a 'fab' spot where I found that I could breathe far more easily. I am affected with the occasional bout of asthma, so this spot was important and a great comfort to me.

I would run my legs off and drink lots and lots of cool water there as I chased after my dreams. In the finer weather, it was so good seeing the flowers swaying in the wind. The trees were large and awesome, and I loved to observe the Serpentine River flowing on and on its way. At the end of the day I would eventually return home exhausted but rested, knowing I would sleep well that night to wake refreshed in the morning.

I mentioned earlier that I visited the Portobello Market with my mum, but on other occasions I went with my brother Michael too. He was keen on collecting stamps and coins. They are fascinating hobbies, although I couldn't fit them into my busy routine—or so I convinced myself at this particular time. Yet it was Michael who introduced me to the joys of playing football and the wonderful game of chess.

It was with great delight that I waited patiently for the Irish Annual Folk Festival which was held at none other than the Porchester Hall. I would get so excited as I waited for the show to begin and as I chilled out with my family and friends. Everyone there was so happy as they laughed and smiled. Nobody seemed to have a care in the world. I think the thought of all the singing and dancing to come had chased all their cares away. I, even felt my toes begin to tap as some familiar melodies floated through my mind. I, like everyone else, was getting into the spirit of it all.

Chapter Two

Do you know what? It's so very strange, but sometimes something happens that almost completely knocks you off your feet. Yes, this happened to myself. It all started when Uncle Paddy out of the blue suddenly approached my family and me at this Irish Concert and said he needed a favour. I liked Uncle Paddy because he had a heart of gold, but he had the reddest face that you could have possibly ever imagined. My Auntie Mae said this was all down to the gallons of booze he had drunk over the years. She quipped he was like a volcano that was just about to blow its top. Uncle Mae said not to tell him though as he didn't like being criticised, and if he heard what she had said about him, he probably wouldn't speak to her for at least three months.

Nevertheless, I was proud that it was my Uncle Paddy who was the main organiser of this Irish Folk Festival. However, as I mentioned, one of the weirdest things then began to occur to me. After my Uncle heartily began to greet everyone, he completely took my breath away by asking me if I would like to open the show with 'a little Irish jig'.

Apparently, a young lad, Dermot O'Leary, the same age as I and who Grandpa said 'could dance the hind legs of a donkey', had gone down with the flu. It was a desperate situation, and didn't I know it. I couldn't believe that I was being put in this position. After all, I had only one dancing lesson to my name.

Unfortunately, Uncle was not hearing any of my objections. He got hold of me like a rabbit in a trap and before you could say 'It's a long way to Tipperary,' I was whisked off double - quick to the changing room. Aye, my protests were all the time being stubbornly ignored. And to make things even worse, the kilt he wanted me to get into was at least three times my size.

My uncle was not prepared to be put off in any way, shape, or form. No, not in the least. He produced a belt out of nowhere as if it was some kind of a magic wand. It was a gigantic looking thing; without a word of a lie, it was at least five, if not six times my waist size. He wrapped it around me, and I felt as if I was being turned into a fattened Christmas turkey, trimmings and all, ready to be served up to an unsuspecting audience. Unfortunately, little did I know this was to be the case.

Before my unprepared self was sent out to an expectant crowd, my uncle noticed my pale complexion and the sweat on my forehead and, not too surprisingly, that I wasn't looking the picture of confidence and health.

'Anyhow, the show has to go on,' he simply pointed out, and added to this by insisting, 'There is nothing really much, no, nothing much at all really to this dancing lark.' And he kept on reassuring me that I had nothing in this world, no, nothing to worry my little head about.

He suggested that everything would be fine if I merely kept in time to the music whilst sprightly dancing around the stage. Yet, he stated, I was not to forget the odd 'high flying' kick when the accompanying music went up a beat or two. Then all, he emphasised, *should* go well.

If only events in life turned out as we wished them to! If only—and if only life was that simple. But, alas, this is not always the case. I went from the changing rooms with my Uncle's 'encouraging' words ringing in my ears—words such as, 'Kevin, go out there and slay the audience with your performance. You'll have them all, one and all, eating out of the palm of your hands.' My favourite was, 'You'll be a star!'

There was an expectant hush as I approached the stage in order to open the concert. Yes, all eyes were fixed on me as soon as I got on the stage, and then the music started up. My grand self began to dance around the stage as if I owned 'the joint', and for a short period of ecstatic time I felt that I was dancing on top of the world—a natural, carefree, and without a worry in the universe. It even occurred to me that Uncle Paddy's words were actually ringing so true and that after all, 'There wasn't really much to this dancing game.'

There was one problem though. This was that the spotlight was shining very brightly into my eyes, and I'm not sure why, but the stage didn't appear to be well lit up at all. What happened next was what I could only describe as unfortunate. Aye, very unfortunate. To be blunt, I fell off the stage. It could well have proved tragic for my person, as well as being extremely painful. Fortunately for myself, there was a miracle in the shape of a mattress placed in front of the stage. To this day, I thank the Good Lord for this saving grace! After a dodgy landing, I was eventually helped back onto the stage by some kind soul, a local nun, Sister Merciful. As for me, I was shaken but not stirred.

I don't want to state the obvious, and as my Auntie Pat would always say, 'you wouldn't have to be Sherlock Holmes' to have noticed that I didn't have the twinkle toes of my friend Dermot. But I did see many of the audience enjoying themselves. Now, let's be honest here, and this is a very important thing. 'Laughter is the best form of medicine,' my grandma would often proclaim. Very important indeed! Someone did point out that some of the audience had actually wet themselves during my performance and had to quickly retreat to the local loos, where there were record queues.

I heard my uncle call from the side of the stage that there was one minute to go before I finished my act. He made it clear to me that he wanted me to do a high flying kick to finish on—a kind of grand and majestic finale. Consequently, I carried out his orders to a tee and lunged like a deer in a field, but upon doing so, my belt gave way, followed by my kilt immediately falling around my ankles. Thank heavens for my y-fronts, because as Grandma pointed out after the show had finished, I could have been arrested for indecent exposure, and that wouldn't do for a young lad at my time of life to be marched off to prison. Grandpa said that if that had occurred, I need not have worried, as he would have come and visited me.

Chapter Three

I was nicknamed 'Kilty-boy' after that particular Irish-folk get-together. I was without doubt one of Ireland's own. The name kind of stuck like superglue. Some of my friends and other folk said that their parents and relatives had never laughed so much in all their entire lives. Afterwards, it was always referred to as the 'M-o-m-e-n-t-o-u-s Festival'. I, though, have always looked back on this event in in a positive and a humorous light. I shall repeat once more that it is of extreme importance that people should always have a smile on their face. It is so important.

Yes, it should be one of the things that folk, young and old, should have on top of their tips for living so they won't develop 'cracked faces.' I heard a wise saying about this. 'Many take life much too seriously and need to adjust their corsets,' Uncle was quick to point out. I had just found out that only women usually wear corsets, and I asked Grandma why Grandpa should say this. She said she didn't know, but if she caught him wearing any of her corsets, she would report him to the police. 'The Lord have mercy on us all!', she said, looking to the heavens for support.

I made friends with a new boy that just moved into the area from the north of England. He was called Billy Brankin. Grandpa called him 'Billy Bandit', because Billy was always getting into trouble. Grandma thought that 'Dennis the Menace' was modelled after him. I am not sure why, but everywhere I went with him, we seemed to end up in double trouble. However, once in a while, this was not the case, and we sometimes enjoyed having a right old belly laugh. One way we did this was by standing outside a local pub called the Shaggy Goat and listening to one of the resident comedians such as Danny O'Driscol. One of my favourite jokes of his goes something like this.

There were an Englishman, Scotsman, Welshman, and Irishman who were taking part in their first parachute jump. The Englishman jumps out of the plane and opens up his parachute and starts to descend to the ground. The same thing happens with the Scotsman as well as the Welshman. When it comes to the Irishman's turn, he leaps wholeheartedly from the plane and as he suddenly goes hurtling by the other three he announces, 'The last one down buys the drinks!'

I had a terrible and fierce fright once. I don't know why, but Ma bought this pair of leather trousers. (I think my teacher, Miss Munroe, said they were called l-e-d-e-r-h-o-s-e-n.) I wasn't too keen on them, but after I eventually got into them, I headed off to school. It was terrible, for when I had to undo them, I couldn't! Thank heavens Miss Munroe helped me. What might have happened? Bits of myself could have been found splattered all over the place. An exploding pillock! I felt like a right banana, I can tell you for nothing.

It was great when we headed off to Ireland for five weeks. I hadn't been outside of England before. Well, I tell a fib. I had been to Kerry in Eire when I was about three years of age. This was where Ma was born. My only memory there was of me leaping about three and a half feet into the air (which was quite something, as I was only about two and a half feet in height) after seeing a large worm as I was coming down a mountain path. I thought it was a small snake. I was duly comforted though by one of my many relatives, who told me that there was nothing to worry about at all as St Patrick had given these critters the boot many years ago.

Well, it would have been very nice if someone had bothered to give me this vital information a little time before I arrived. For sure, it would have been only fair to have done so. Also, it might have helped stop my pounding heart from leaping straight into my mouth at the time. Added to this, it could have saved my none-too-pleased mother the trouble of changing my none-too-clean underwear.

However, this time we visited County Waterford in Eire, where my Dad came from. I love Ireland—the green fields and lovely cottages. Everyone is so friendly and loving—to me myself anyway. I loved the women folk there especially when they made a fuss over me. They gave me lots and lots of hugs and kisses and tons of sweets and cups of scrummy hot chocolate.

One of my uncles in Waterford had left his two-bedroomed cottage and a half an acre of land in return for a loan my pa had given him. In the field a beautiful one-eyed horse named Dolly resided. She was lovely, and one day my Uncle Paul mounted Maureen and myself on her back for an exciting ride. It was like sitting on the top of a skyscraper. Unexpectedly, the horse bolted! Maureen hung onto Dolly and I hung onto Maureen, before Dolly calmed down. What a ride! However, not for the fainthearted.

Another highlight, apart from visiting all my relatives, was going to the pictures. It's 'brill' that there are no age restrictions in Eire for viewing films. I saw my first X-rated film about Dracula when I was seven years. Yes, I must admit that it was rather scary. I shall never forget how the movie opened with blood gradually trickling down Dracula's gravestone, and as it continued to do so, my sister Maureen at the same time slid under her seat until she was completely out of view.

'Scaredy cat! Scaredy cat!' I said to her, but I didn't really mean it. Oh, yes I did! (Only joking!)

Dracula was a strange dude. If you ask me, I would say he was a bit on the loony side. And it goes without saying that he was not everyone's cup of tea. When he had sunk his fangs into many a fair young maiden, Grandpa quipped, 'Fangs aren't what they used to be!' Everyone laughed.

I was so sorry when my family and I had to leave the Emerald Isle, but that is how life is at times—unfair. However, I was so grateful to have this welcome break. Everyone needs one, old and young, young and old. Grandpa says all of us need to stop and 'charge our batteries' every now and then.

There were so many interesting and 'different' folk that lived around Notting Hill of course, too many for me to mention. However, a few come to mind whom I will tell you about. 'Bonzie' was a local tough who to me looked a bit like Frankenstein (bolts and fittings included, and all)! It went without saying that if anyone had any sense, they should keep their distance from him. I didn't really like him because I thought he was a bit of a bully, and I, like many a fair-minded person, don't like bullies in any way, shape, or form.

Helen's mother Peggy was another unforgettable person who resided here. Although she was small in stature, she was forever scrapping with her much bigger spouse and coming out looking like she had been fighting for the boxing heavyweight championship of the world. (None too successfully, may I add?) Peggy would be endlessly heard calling one of her four children names. On such occasions her voice would manage to hit such a high note that my mate Billy said it sounded like she had just sat on a large needle! This, without doubt, caused the sharp pitch in her voice to rise sensationally!

Last but not least, there was the one and only Mr Mulloney. He was a big and 'prehistoric' character, rough to be sure. I called him 'Mr Rhino Bum' because when he was having a fight with someone—which was often at one of the local pubs—he would begin to wrestle his opponent to the ground and then proceed to sit on the poor chap's face. Umm . . . I agree, it was a strange and odd thing to do. Billy said it was especially bad for the unfortunate victim if Mr Mulloney had just eaten a king-size curry the night before! Evidence of this was soon to become very apparent when the victim in this uncompromising position would soon proceed to go a subtle green in the face! Yipes!

Chapter Four

The main form of heating in our flat was coal. There were a few electric fires dotted around here and there, but because my parents said they were too expensive to use, we rarely put them on. And the only coal fireplace that was in use here 'in our palace' was in our living room on the second floor. As you would expect, it got mighty cold in the winter, and this would cause us all to sit right down almost on top of the fire. Owing to this, we would get an odd red colouring on our legs which Ma would refer to as 'the lazy ABC'. I was never quite sure why she would say this, but she did. We got the coal from a coalman that came around our area in his van.

Some visiting folk to our neighbourhood were quite shocked that we still had gas lighting in our streets. I once heard an American tourist remark, 'This patch looks like something out of the Dickens era. It's a son-of-a-gun time-warp!'

Helen revealed one day that she would like to play doctors and nurses. I told her about my episode with Carol, but she wasn't in the least bit put off. She wanted to play so much that I couldn't say no to her. Well, you can't, can you, when any girl insists so much and endlessly goes on at you?

Anyhow, we both got dressed up for the part. Helen confided in me that this was very important to her. She had made up her mind that she had decided that she wanted to be a nurse and that she desired to be nothing else. Her calling, without a shadow of a doubt she was sure, was to look after the frail and the sick whether they were young or old. How could I, a young Irish lad, deny such a request from a fair and determined maiden? Not me. After all, I've always wanted to do my bit for suffering mankind.

Wow! It was brilliant when I was dressed up as a 'mummy'. Oh sorry, I mean as a doctor. And Helen, for her part, was splendid in her get-up as a nurse. After some time, we found a deserted room around the corner in Moorehouse Road where we could make our fancy dress really come to life. However, there was one thing at this time that I did find a little strange. This was all the candles that Helen had lit and placed around our 'medical' room. She informed me that there were simply there to add some 'atmosphere' to our role-play.

Anyway, we were just about getting into our stride, when Helen accidentally knocked over one of the candles, and before anyone could say 'What the Dickens!' the whole bloomin' flat began to go up in flames! It was a nightmare. The fire brigade turned up. Then Helen's mum, upon hearing what had occurred, went into one of her out-of-this-world 'supersonic' tones. Fortunately for both of us, Helen and myself, we were dramatically rescued, but only in the nick of time. 'The medical pair,' as uncle Mike referred to us, emerged looking like two very scorched and over-cooked turkeys coming out of the Christmas oven.

This was not the festive season, as Helen's mum Peggy blamed everything on me. How unreasonable can some people be? Added to this, to put it mildly, Pa was more than annoyed that I was still playing doctors and nurses. If looks could have turned someone to stone, Pa was your man! Margaret, I thought, unfairly stated that she was going to send me straight away to see a psychiatrist—me being only seven years old after all! (I nearly forgot to mention that when I was rescued by the firemen, I was feeling so embarrassed that my cheeks began to glow like two red hot coals—and I can still feel them glowing!)

My Auntie Maud considered that many people had a problem for all kinds of reasons with discharging wind. (Some folk felt that she was a pioneer of worldwide hygiene.) She announced that it would be a great aid to each and every one on this planet if some bright 'Einstein' could invent what could be called 'a posterior muffler'. Straight up!

Auntie went on to say that this device should have a twofold effect. First, it should completely muffle the noise of the passing wind. Second, and this was even more important, it should at the same time take away the smell. She felt so strongly about this that she even went so far as to imply that it might lead to the possible salvation of mankind—a heaven on earth, if you like. It would, at the least, free many sensitively-nosed people from the many 'bad-air zones'. Grandpa felt a wee bit exasperated when he heard her remarks and pointed out that Auntie Maud had more than a tendency to exaggerate. He declared that in her case 'the lights are on, but there is definitely nobody at home.'

I decided all by myself to go to my first confession. It did seem the right thing to do at the time. I was feeling very nervous as I wasn't used to talking to a complete stranger, whether it was a priest or not. I meekly entered into the confessional box, thinking at the time that it was as dark as hell itself. It seemed an eternity before the shutter, separating myself from the priest, opened. I don't wish to sound disrespectful, but when he appeared he looked so old—at least one hundred and twenty-five years old to be precise. Added to this, he hardly appeared to be moving at all. Had he just passed on, I thought to myself, or was he having a hard day listening to sinners like myself and had decided to have a quick nap? You couldn't blame him though. Well, reaching one hundred and twenty-five is a great age, to be sure it is. I thought only giant tortoises got to such an age. I made up my mind I would come back another day, and I was just about to leave when a very deep and croaky voice spoke to me.

'How long has it been since your last confession, my boy?'

'I've never been before, Father.'

'Why not?'

'Well . . .'

'Are you having me on, my lad?'

He looked at me, and I'm not telling you a word of a lie, as if he was going to murder myself. I fled. I felt I had no choice. I hadn't quite made up my mind when I would return, possibly . . . umm . . . never! Grandpa said he always had his suspicions about holy people as they often appear so intense. I don't like intense people. They are scary.

I prayed to St Jude. Sister Magdalene, a nun from the local convent, told me all about him. He is the patron saint of hopeless causes. I am not too sure why, but I have sort of adopted him as a cool dude that can help me out of any jam. I like saints.

I said a prayer for Godfrey, a goldfish I recently purchased at the pet shop. He all of a sudden died and just started floating around the top of my fish bowl, a bit like me in the swimming pool. Thankfully I am not dead, but Godfrey's time had come. I asked Pa what had happened to Godfrey. Pa thought for a while and came to the conclusion that he had drowned.

It will come as no surprise at all that my friend Billy got me in hot soup again. I was minding my own business whilst counting my pennies after returning pop bottles to the off-license, when he approached me. I was feeling on the thirsty side, as the sun was 'cracking the stones' as my cousin Annie was likely to say. He was rather breathless as he informed me that the local lover boy 'Hot Lips Benny' was kissing one the local girls 'Busty Betty' on a bench in her backyard. He pointed out that if I stood on his back, I would be able to get 'an eyeful' or a bird's eye view of them doing what lovers do. Something inside my head told me that I shouldn't have bothered, especially, if Billy was involved. But I did.

He was bending down and telling me that if I didn't get on his back and look over the wall, he would make it known to everyone that I was a scaredy cat! Anyway, I climbed onto his back and discovered Busty Betty and Hot Lips Billy looking like a pair of cooing lovebirds, kissing and whispering what my sister Eileen had referred to as 'sweet nothings'. Urgh! Uck!

Billy kept on asking me what the two lovebirds were doing as if it was some kind of grown - up mystery. In the meantime, a policeman passed by and noticed Billy and me. He didn't need to be Sherlock Holmes either to put two and two together. When Billy noticed the Law running towards us, he decided to do a runner himself, leaving yours truly spread all over the pavement like a sack of spuds as he did so. As I descended, I let out a yelp, only for Betty and Benny, unfortunately, to clap their eyes on me! I heard them calling out my name as I fled into the distance. I could just make out the two lovey-doves shouting after me that they were going to tell my parents that I was a peeping tom and also give my details to the policeman whom I had managed to give the slip.

In the circumstances, I decided to lie low as Betty and Billy were on the warpath. It crossed my mind it might be an ideal time to move as far away from home as was humanly possible. Now let me think . . . hmm . . . Australia . . . maybe? I daren't repeat what they said they would do if they laid hands on poor old sensitive me. Not on your nelly.

Chapter Five

One thing that I liked about living in Notting Hill was all the different cultures that resided here. This was really good because it made life so much more interesting. Miss Hughes told us kids at school that variety is the spice of life, and the Notting Hill Carnival brought all the splendid elements of the world onto the colourful streets of my neighbourhood. I loved to see the happy, smiling faces of the adults as well as the little folk. The music and the costumes are 'electric', as my brother would comment. My vote for a best costume would be a West Indian girl dressed up as a blue and gold butterfly. Her wings would shine bright like the sun as she floated down the road. Also, and very importantly, there was great 'nosh' and drink on offer for us lucky ones.

Yes, every colour of the rainbow was on display, shining for everyone to see. It was great to see so many people dancing. I loved to dance, even if my sister Rita considered that I looked a little out of rhythm. Michael pointed out that at the carnival, people were 'letting it all hang out'—whatever that meant! My sister Eileen said this event was 'groovy', as did my sister Maureen who was often in charge of looking after me.

I was lucky enough to be chosen as Joseph, Jesus' earthly Pa, in the school nativity play. I really enjoyed myself immensely as I was acting with my classmates, even though I kept on forgetting my lines. Everyone laughed at me doing so, and I have rarely seen so many tears of joy rolling down folks' faces. I would say there was about the same amount of laughter as on the fateful evening at Porchester Hall when I was given my nickname of 'Kilty-boy'. Some were even shouting 'encore' when I left the stage at the end of the nativity play. Ma gave me a big hug afterwards and told me how proud she was of me and also informed me how much she loved me. Therefore, that made everything so very worthwhile.

There is a photograph of me in the nativity play. I am standing on the left as Joseph with Madeleine, my new girlfriend, on the right. The baby Jesus is in the middle. He is a small doll and not a real baby. Mrs MacArthur, the headmistress at my school, said we could not have a real baby as there was a real danger I might accidentally drop it!

Billy was being held at the local police station. The latest 'brainer' he had come up with was to knock off a policeman's helmet and then disappear before the policeman had realised what had happened. The thrill was . . . well, eh . . . not getting caught . . . umm . . . However, to be fair, he did put his own brainer to the test as he proceeded to go out and detach an unsuspecting policeman from his helmet. Of course, he then made a frantic dash for it. However, this wicked scheme didn't quite go to plan as he was arrested straight away on the corner of the same street by a burly police sergeant who just happened to witness what Billy had done

He was about to be let off with a warning 'to behave himself in the future'. Policemen don't take too kindly to having their helmets removed from their person—who would?—especially if they don't give their permission for someone to do so in the first place. Alas, the cops were soon to change their minds and keep him at the police station a bit longer when something else occurred. It was a tragedy, and it all went pear-shaped when Billy suddenly asked, 'What do you think of the idea of a bunch of fives straight up a policeman's hooter?' Unsurprisingly, they didn't think too much of this new idea either, and they were now keeping him in for further questioning with his mother and father in attendance. I liked Billy, but I came to the obvious conclusion: Billy is bleedin' well bonkers!

Chapter Six

One of the great joys of life is eating my meals with my family. It is not always possible because everyone seems to have to do their own particular things at different times. However, Sunday afternoon is often a great time 'for sharing and breaking bread' as Father McCarthy from my school often quotes. My mum makes it the best meal of the week and always cooks a Sunday roast. Yummy! Soup is served first. This is something we don't usually have during the week. However, Sunday is an exception. On that day, Ma makes roast beef or roast chicken, roast or mashed potatoes, a few vegetables, and Yorkshire pudding as well. To top it all, we have piping-hot gravy. Super! For afters, we usually have a lovely pudding, which is often trifle. I love puddings. There are so many puddings I like that I could fill up pages to tell you all of them. Therefore, jam roly-poly and chocolate fudge pudding will give you some idea.

Pa usually says grace, but sometimes it is Ma or my brother or one of my three sisters. If we have a guest, he or she usually says it. Thankfully, grace doesn't take too long, as I sometimes get starving hungry looking at all the glorious grub on display. Once I ate a piece of a small roast potato before we had started the meal, and Ma slapped my wrist and scolded me and told me to be patient. Pa gave one of his looks and sternly uttered to me. 'Any more bad manners like that, and I know someone who could be joining Billy at the police station!' Surely not!

After the meal we can chat and laugh together and be thankful that we feel so good. We talk about so many things that I would be here to the next century if I were to let you know what they all were. So I will save it for another day. Younger ones like me drink orange juice or cola. The grownups like beer and wine, apart from Ma, who only drinks alcohol at Christmas. She has a drink that was called 'a snowball'. It seems a funny name to call a drink, but I guess I suppose that grown - up folk are a bit funny after all.

I like it when Grandma and Grandpa visit for Sunday lunch. They often bring bars of chocolate with them to my ever grateful self. They have been married for so long that they say that they can't remember how long. I think they are only kidding me though, as they often say that they cherish every day that they have spent together. It could be that when folk get older, their memory goes a bit dodgy. Anyway, they just told me once again that I was a special gift from God. How lovely! And they are so blessed to have me as their precious grandson.

I love them both, too, even though they look 'as old as the hills'. I look up to them both, and I want to be as loving and generous as they are when I get big. They are constantly telling me I am growing up. They asked me what I wanted to be when I was a man. I told them right away that I wanted to be a butterfly. They looked at each other and smiled and then lovingly looked at myself and said, 'How nice!'

I love walking around the Portobello Road and up to Ladbroke Grove and further on to Latymer Road. On other occasions I might go in a different direction and amble up the Great Western Road that passes Westbourne Park Road underground station, all the way up to the long and winding Harrow Road. Now and again, I walk to the Bayswater Road and go to Oxford Street, which I find is quite exciting but a bit overwhelming for a little lad like myself. All the same, I like the atmosphere and like to observe so many shoppers getting so much pleasure out of shopping.

Older people now seem to be always changing their hairstyle as well as their clothing in one way or another and trying out new food and drink as well. Mrs MacArthur says that life is always changing and when I get much older I will understand this fact a lot more than I do now. I will look forward to that . . . I think. I hope I can understand others as they sometimes act so mean towards each other. 'People are sometimes strange,' Grandma used to say. 'I think they act in the way that they do because deep down they are often unhappy.' I like Grandma.

I forgot to mention that Michael, Eileen, Rita, and I take after Ma with our brown hair and eyes. However, Maureen takes after Pa with her blonde hair and blue eyes. My mother is a little over five feet and is built like a battleship, as some neighbours have remarked. My father is about five foot and ten inches. Ma tells me I get my good looks from her. Right on! Grandma and Grandpa are old and grey and to me they look like they have been living forever.

I love pop music, Elvis Presley especially. It is nice to hear so many good pop groups appearing, such as the Beatles and the Rolling Stones. We are a family that loves all kinds of music, including folk and classical. For sure, there is nothing quite like a good song and a fine tune to get the toes and fingers tapping. Eileen's favourite singer is the American crooner Pat Boone. I am sure she secretly loves him and would like to marry him if she could. I am certain she also thinks he is the best thing since sliced bread with chocolate spread all over it. Eileen, however, keeps her thoughts to herself because she doesn't want everyone locally to consider her to be some kind of eejit. Rock on!

Not only do the grown - ups go to pubs and clubs these days, but they like to visit the trendy coffee shops that are springing up like shamrocks. Rita states that these are considered 'hip', as well as everything else going on. Grandpa has even been and liked it as he met an old pal from Ireland, Dennis Sullivan, from his boyhood. Dennis apparently jumped on board a ship leaving Ireland for America when he was only twelve years of ageing. He had no choice, as there were another thirteen siblings in his family, and his parents just couldn't cope and feed them all in those days. This was a time when many folk hadn't two brass farthings to rub together. I wasn't sure how they recognised each other as it was about sixty years or so since Dennis took his mighty step. Maybe these days people are not aging anymore. Grandpa and Dennis had a great ol' meeting though. It was a 'top of the morning' for the both of them, so Grandpa stated. And it came as no surprise to me at any rate that they went on to a place where the drink was a wee bit stronger.

Myself and Billy were standing outside a pub called the Creepy Caterpillar the other day in order to listen to a new Irish comedian named Dusty Delaney. Every time Dusty opens his mouth to tell a joke, everyone, including myself and Billy, rolls about on the floor in uncontrollable fits of laughter. And to give you some idea what I am talking about, I have try to remember one of his cracks or jokes.

A man comes home and finds his wife with another man. The husband proclaims with great annoyance to his wife, 'What are you doing with that horse?'

25

The wife turns to her lover and says, 'For sure, I have told you before that this husband of mine urgently needs to go and see Specsavers!'

I've taken to completing jigsaws these days. It's a great way to pass the time. I get lost in the magic of it all. And there's nothing more wonderful—and that gives me a marvellous sense of satisfaction—than when I eventually manage to complete it. If it happens to be a very huge jigsaw, it can take me for what seems like forever and ever, but I don't care. Sometimes I take so long to complete it that Pa says that 'the cows will soon be coming home'. I find this rather confusing as there are no cows around these parts.

Auntie May dropped a lovely vase around at her place recently and said it broke into a million and one pieces. I assumed by what she uttered that it couldn't be mended. It's a pity, really, when a tube of sticky glue can do miracles. I thought she would be very pleased when I informed her of this, but she rather crossly told me to 'stick to jigsaw puzzles and stop "addling" and annoying me.' Well, I have discovered that this is what happens in life sometimes when you *try* to be helpful!

Chapter Seven

I invited my friend Sean from my school to play 'flick' football with me at my place. This was a game with tiny plastic footballers on a green piece of cloth—that is, a football pitch—with goalposts, football markings, and all. The aim is to flick the tiny football into the goal, via the plastic footballers of course. He very kindly gave it to me as a birthday present, so I thought I should try to do something as a kind of thank you.

He is not from round my patch but from the posh area of Chelsea in southwest London. Yes, he is from a well-off family and lives in a lovely place with a fantastic garden and all. I know because I visited him once. His Dad picked me up from the Gardens and dropped me back to the Palace later. I asked Sean why he didn't go to a local school in Chelsea. He replied that his parents considered themselves 'trendy and liberal' and they wanted him to experience 'the other side of life'. I didn't quite understand what he meant at first, but eventually, after my sister Rita explained it to me, I did. I like people that are trendy and liberal. I think.

I must point out that this idea of him visiting me was already turning out to be a huge mistake. I realized it as soon as Sean arrived. He had not been to my home before. However, I knew by the look on his face that it would be not only the first time but, alas, the last. He hadn't even set foot inside the front door, and it might seem strange, but his complexion appeared to be going a subtle shade of green.

After we greeted each other, he began to sniff aloud as if he was smelling something quite strange. Myself, I am used to the odours as I was brought up there. Yet, it did occur to me that he could be smelling 'the sweet odours' of the family in the basement, or the slightly nearer pongs from the lot situated on the ground floor, or possibly both. Then, for some unknown reason, I had the feeling that Sean and I were in some kind of war-zone. I thought I was acting extremely wisely when I told him to hold his breath, before we both started to dash up the stairs to the second floor where Ma was waiting for us.

Events became even odder when, after reaching the living room with Sean, my mother asked me why my friend was looking green—an easy mistake to make, as folk don't usually go green. Sean asked if he could have some water. My mum fetched him some and advised him to lie down. I must admit, and I'm being very honest now, that I did feel sorry for him. I did. Nevertheless, I was a bit sorry for myself as well, as it was very, very disappointing that we never got around to playing flick football. I had, even decided to throw the match to allow Sean to win at flick football. Well, it was the least I could do as I was host.

Thankfully, he got home okay. I couldn't quite put my finger on it, but we have never been quite as close since his visit. My brother Michael quipped, 'Maybe your friend didn't like seeing "the other side of life".' Maybe.

My young love life has received, yet again, another big bashing. First, Carol never seems to have much time for me anymore and has revealed that she prefers older and more 'mature' boys of about eight or nine years of age. Second, Peggy, Helen's mum, had warned me off her daughter, blaming me for the 'medical room blaze' and not only that but for also being the main cause of her beloved baby girl looking like 'a scalded cat'! Charming! Third, and last but not least, the new love of my life, Madeleine, who played Mary alongside me in the nativity play has just returned a bracelet I gave her—it cost tuppence, by the way—pledging that she has decided to see me no more as she had made up her mind that she is going to become a nun.

I think I might give up on this subject until I get a bit older. Girls have always been a mystery to me. And when I asked my Grandma why there are so many young women around our area with very short skirts, loads of make-up on, and always seeming to be hanging around street corners, she said I would do better if I didn't concern myself with such matters and concentrate on my schoolwork instead, as well as reading the Bible. Maybe, she pointed out, I should sing a song from the Celtic paper *Ireland's Own*. This would be following the example of my 'songbird' Ma, who was always singing songs from it.

There's a really laid-back musician in our area called Jeremiah. 'Praise Jah!' he would constantly say. He said it was the Hebrew for 'Praise the living and Almighty God.' I sometimes hang out with him when he is having a coffee with his mates. Actually, I don't really hang out with him. I sort of tag along because like to hear him speak. Jeremiah doesn't seem to mind. One of the songs he plays as he sings is called 'How can I write it?' The song is lovely. The chorus goes, 'How can I write it? How can I say it? How can I tell you . . . I love you?' I think he is a nice and a friendly person.

'True humility is the sign of a great man.' Tim Buckley, an elderly neighbour who is a friend of the family, is giving everybody a good quote. If you want a good quote, it is widely known around our parts, Tim is your man. He said we were originally like 'the salt of the earth', but asking some folk to change was like asking 'pigs to fly'! He said more than anything that he wanted to be remembered as a man who had *soul*.

'Time is a great healer.' Auntie May has just finished saying her Rosary. She got up from the floor. 'Do you know, I heard a great saying the other day? I think it is a Chinese proverb. "Life begins on the day you start a garden." Remember that, garcoon, as one day you might become a writer.'

'Most certainly, Auntie May. I really love gardens,' I heartily reply.

'Remember the starving children in Africa.' My parents would always remind me of that stark fact if I happened to leave any food on my plate after a meal. Do you know what? If I ruled the world, I would give everyone enough to eat and drink. My folks said that I was not to worry or fret about big and mighty matters as there are many things beyond us, especially beyond smaller people like me. However, I was encouraged by them to continue to trust and believe in Him.

'Tempus Fugit!' (time flies) is one of my favourite sayings, and 'It is better to be born lucky than rich' is another. My very favourite is 'Love never fails.' This is a corker! And I am reminded of an old Irish one that goes . . .

'May your roof never fall in, and with your friends, may you never fall out!'

I am going once more up onto the roof in order to let all my cares and worries sort themselves out. 'Take one blessed step at a time,' Sister Magdalene always advised me, 'and put your best foot forward.' At last I feel way down inside myself that I am running wild and free.

Father Matthews made a visit to my Bible-study classes last weekend. He was very encouraging as well as being inspirational to all of us kids that were attending there. He knew heaps and heaps about the Bible. Ma referred to his knowledge as being 'a right royal treasure trove.' My ex-girlfriend Madeleine enquired of the priest what was his favourite Bible story. Father Matthews paused for a short instance whilst stroking his chin in deep contemplation before revealing it was the story concerning the prophet of old, Elijah. He informed us that this good and holy man was being persecuted terribly by his own people who did not like him telling them the truth. It got to such a bad stage that he was in serious danger of being done away with. However, God rescued him, as he empowered Elijah to fly up to the heavens in his chariot in order that he would be safe forever.

Hey! I thought that was a great and inspirational story.

And do you know what? I don't know about you, but I would love to ascend up to the starry skies one day. Cor, without a shadow of a doubt that would really be the tops for me. Bullseye! For sure, I would love to see that blessed day. Certainly. Breaking the sound barrier would be no problem. Easy-peasy. A great example of hitting the heights, don't you think? However, in my particular case I would most definitely make sure that I was reinforced with my crash helmet on—for safety reasons, of course!

Aye, for sure, after all my travelling has come to an end along my long and winding road, I've decided that there could be no more blessed and tantalising chant than 'To the stars . . .'

Chapter Eight

'Throw in a sprat to catch a mackerel!' Uncle Tommy was the tops for coming up with sporting quotes . . . especially the 'fishy' ones.

Paddington, in Notting Hill, breathes another sigh of relief as one more day dawns. It's strange, but here in winter a kind of mist descends as if a cloud is waiting to be lifted. It pervades like a silent witness in my home. It lingers on the road and the railings and somehow clings to the billboards that depict events that hope to enliven our lives. I am now thirteen years of age, and even I am becoming aware of how time flies.

'Life is a rollercoaster, but don't forget that the most important thing for folk to do is to enjoy the ride and to take time to stop and smell the flowers.' Melissa, Eileen's pretty hippie friend, plays with the beads in her long blonde hair as she gives the impression that the world belongs solely to her. And maybe it does.

My simple existence continues . . . and the sights, sounds, and smells have changed very little. And to me the actual thought and the realisation that I live in what some would describe as a slum is of no great importance at all.

Ma and Pa are working hard as usual. They have scrimped and saved for years in order to send Michael, my brother, off to university. He chose to go to St Andrews in Dundee in bonny Scotland. He is studying for a Bachelor of Science in Mathematics. He is the clever one of the family. I believe St Andrews is the home of golf. I am sure that Uncle Tommy, given time, will come up with a 'sporty' quote shortly—corny, but good for a laugh nevertheless. But in the meantime, I shall move on.

Eileen, the eldest of my sisters, is now working in the post office as a clerk, Rita is training to be a nurse, and Maureen is finishing her schooling at Cardinal Manning Girls' School in Ladbroke Grove. Me, I am in my third year in my secondary school at the London Oratory in Chelsea. Bob 'the man' Dylan sings that 'the times they are a changin'', Melissa says, but it must be said that anyone would have to be blind not to have noticed this.

'Survival is the key. Life is what you make it.' Grandpa was not only a great believer in home truths but also in being able to stand up for yourself. His other great belief was being an advocate of hard and satisfying work. 'Folk need to have the opportunity to earn their own bread. It is a vital need in their lives in order to give them purpose and dignity.'

All of London, if not almost everywhere, in the mid-1960s seemed to be opening up for me anyway and for my pal Billy Brankin. 'Existence is for living' was a sentiment heard ever on every street corner and alleyway. My friend Billy and I liked to get out and about. We shared the opinion of many other young people. 'You only live once, so it's a time to be alive and kickin'!'

'Put a sock in it, Kevin Barry! You are forever croaking about one thing or the flamin' other!' Mr O'Shea, the resident of the ground floor flat at 98 St Stephen's Gardens, was showing me he didn't appreciate my dulcet tones. Myself, as usual, I was in full voice as I slid athletically down the bannisters, where I quickly arrived in the hallway outside Mr O'Shea's front door before I exited. Grandpa said, when I told him about this incident, that Mr O'Shea was giving me 'the bird.' Some people!

'If you can't say a good word about someone, don't bother saying anything at all!' Cousin Annie was making a comment in passing one day, but upon hearing what Annie had to say, Uncle Paddy quips, 'In all probability, for folks to apply this, there is, in fact, more of a chance that pigs will fly!'

Do you ever feel like you have to scream? I do. I really do. Yet I also like to counteract this. As a matter of fact, I read in the newspaper the other day something on this very subject. This paper reported that in Japan over-stressed and frustrated businessmen in their office environment go into a specially kept room where there is a punching bag. Whereupon, if they happen to feel below par, they proceed to punch the flamin' smithereens out of the unfortunate punch bag until they feel a lot, lot better. Cor! What a great and a 'splendiferous' idea!

Much of my own recreational life is still based in the Back. I've lost count of how many goals I've scored playing football out there. It is probably some kind of a world record, I am sure. The Back is surrounded by four streets—Ledbury Road to the north, Moorehouse Road to the south, St Stephen's Gardens to the east, and Westbourne Park Road to the west.

It is just as well that Ledbury Road looks right down on the Back from the northerly direction, because this is where Granny Hawkins resides, a formidable lady of medium and wiry stature. Apparently, she possesses such an intense look that it was reported it could stop traffic in its tracks. 'Harum-scarum' Hawkins is the unofficial spokeswoman for the area. She watches every little thing like an old buzzard perched in her nest from her first-floor flat. If she doesn't like something that is going on in her patch, she immediately descends like some kind of a bird of prey to air her forthright views.

Maybe I am being a little unfair on her, as she does a lot of good on many occasions on a practical level. Aye, this is when she helps gets rid of any 'riff raff' that try to enter from outside into our own personal domain. Okay, I suppose she could also be referred to as an unelected or self-elected guardian. And in these particular circumstances I have no problem with her at all.

Ma was an indomitable person in her own way too—built like a battleship but at the same time a little quiet and reserved. Granny Hawkins could be as brash as brash can be—a bit full on for my liking. However, I have noticed that people like this are very useful in getting points of view to be heard. And sometime voices need to be heard in order to get anything done.

In contrast to Harum-Scarum, there was a beautiful old lady who lived opposite me, across the road in St Stephen's Gardens. Her name was Angela. She had the sweetest and kindest face you could have possibly imagined. This was complemented by the fact that she had long flowing grey hair. Some of us kids called her 'Angela the Angel' because she was always throwing sweets down from her second-floor flat in the street to us ever-grateful children. (What a heavenly idea!) She had also such a warm, generous, and lovely smile, and I was certain, even though she not fully aware, that her acts of kindness would always mean such a lot to us local children.

Unfortunately, there is often what is termed 'a fly in the ointment'. This is when there is something bad that spoils a good thing. In this case, it was her rather devious and dodgy landlord, who was trying to get her out of her residence. One tactic he used was to try to get her to pay much more rent than she could possibly afford. This type of person (by this I mean unscrupulous) even resorted to harassing this lovely old dear, and he even descended to making lewd comments and noises right outside of her besieged flat. It turned out to be an intolerable situation for harassed Angela to bear. Thus she felt that she had no alternative but to simply leave.

I've said it before and I will say it once more: I detest bullies. My theory is similar to that of Grandpa's—that these very unhappy and sad people seem to get some kind of perverse 'pleasure' by spreading their unhappiness to others. 'Some people are never content unless they make others discontent,' Grandma remarked, 'as if there is not enough going on . . .'

It was such a sorrowful day for each and every one in the Gardens when distraught Angela left her flat forever in order to go into a nursing home. Lots of people, especially us children, turned out in force to wish 'Angela the Angel' all the very best sincerely from our hearts and to assure her that her acts of love will be remembered joyfully by one and all for all time.

I had the weirdest dream the other night. It centred around that famous painting by none other than that chap who has a name like a candy bar. I think you are familiar with the one I mean. The artist is Munch, and the painting was 'The Scream'. The alarming thing about all of this was that I myself portrayed the poor bloke who was the central character in the painting. You know the chap I mean—the geezer who looks like he has just been plugged into the electric mains. No joke. What made things much worse was that I looked even worse than this guy did.

Chapter Nine

It was now the era of the hippies, mods and rockers, beatniks, the ban-the-bomb-brigade, and other kinds of 'cool cats' trying to put the world right as they expressed themselves. (I love a bit of self-expression. I really do.) Yet, at the same time, I am not forgetting to mention the odd 'weirdo', as Eileen sometimes would refer to some of the less-than-ordinary folk that drifted in and out of our neighbourhood.

Ma would quip and joke that the outfits that these lads and lassies were wearing were straight from the wardrobe of a travelling circus. Who knows? Ma had always kept a keen eye on such social matters! It's a pity that she couldn't find time to keep a diary. She was always pointing out that there was many a tale she could tell each and every one that went on down through the decades right here in West London. What a bobby dazzler that would have turned out to be!

Of course, all kinds of happenings were going on at this time. However, there were one or two things she wasn't too happy or enthusiastic about either. To put it mildly, the introduction of the infamous mini-skirt was not top of her favourites list. This apparent symbol of fashion and freedom Ma quirkily described as 'an oversized belt that was wrapped round a shameless young girl's bottom'.

For me the times were certainly changin'. I've never seen so many multi-coloured outfits and pairs of shoes in all my life as were crammed, row upon row, into our small flat. It often looked like we were hosting our very own fashionable 'swingin' sale'. I considered putting a sign outside the house and continually calling out, 'Roll up! Roll up!' I eventually decided against it, but only just . . .

I built this super snowman in the winter. It was the first time I attempted to do so. When the snow came, I often had a terrific time conducting snowball fights with my friends and 'enemies' in the Back and in the park—celestial white heaven! On top of this, I tried to be a wee bit inventive when I used any old wooden crate I could find as a sledge to slide down a hill or indeed any uneven piece of ground.

Nonetheless, above all of this fun and frivolity, Bertie the snowman was ultimately my pride and joy. Without a shadow of a doubt, he really was. Aye, I was so proud to hear him being referred to as 'a real toff'. This was, believe it or not, reportedly said by some senior military guy who had just moved into the area. How splendid!

Bertie had a somewhat large head and, of course, a larger body. 'Chunky' was a term that naturally came to mind. Certainly, great care was taken in his creation. You can be sure of that. For starters, I skilfully placed two large buttons in his head for his eyes and followed this with a zip for his smiling mouth. Also, I expertly placed, to create a super effect, an old school cap of mine on his stately head. Yes, he was most definitely taking shape. Nonetheless, to top it all—and this was my pure touch of genius as well as Bertie's crowning glory—a very large carrot was used to represent his nose. Superb!

Tragically, my pride and joy Bertie only lasted for no more than a few miserable days. Yes, this occurred all too soon, before his 'cool' mystique finally and sadly faded away. It was a terrible time for me as well as for poor ol' Bertie. I suppose it would have been apt if Mr Carter, my English teacher, had quoted at this point something like 'the fleeting life of a passing flower' as a kind of . . . umm . . . 'snowman's requiem'.

Sad to say, life can be so cruel and heartless. Yes it can be. Soon the rot had well and truly set in after a sprightly Yorkshire terrier named Sparkle suddenly took a liking to poor ol' Bertie's carrot nose, and with a mighty leap, this mischievous canine wrenched my poor ol' snowman's hooter right off his mush, before disappearing with it, never to be seen again.

Following these unforeseen events, the weather then got much worse. Well, to be precise in the circumstances, it unexpectedly got warmer—quite a bit warmer, actually. And eventually poor ol' Chunky Bertie turned into nothing more than one of helluva of a great big fat watery blob.

Alas, there was not much evidence remaining of poor ol' Bertie's ultra-brief and glorious existence, let me tell you, apart from the only concrete evidence remaining of him—my soggy primary school cap.

My brother Michael was a wizard at doing tricks with a football. I mean he could keep it up dozens of times on each foot, on each thigh, on his head for ages, and the superb finale was that he would get the ball to rest on the back of his neck. He was a maestro. Nearly everyone was amazed at his skill, and sometimes in the street he would have a small crowd gather around to watch him. I was really, really proud of him.

Myself, I tried my best to equal Michael and show off some of my own football skills, but I just couldn't quite match him. I suppose, I mused, that I would have to resign myself to the comforting thought that my strength lay in the fact that I was potentially the greatest goal-scorer that the world had ever seen. Well, that's my own story, and I am flamin' well sticking to it anyway.

Do you know what? I think we have one of the heaviest blokes in the whole of Great Britain and Eire, and that chap resides in none other than Notting Hill Gate itself? It's a fact! This chap is known locally as 'Little Willie'. Nevertheless, I can truthfully confess that my heart goes out to him as he weighs over fifty stone and has just been renamed 'Hippo Bum' by none other than Billy, my mate. Ultimately, when all is said and done, one could only feel the greatest sorrow for this larger-than-life character though.

For instance, last weekend Hippo Bum—sorry, Little Willie—got stuck in his bath. It was one hell of a job to shift him, or so I have been told. Aye, to be sure, it apparently leaked out that he had to be manfully wedged out after a few hours by the none other than the local fire brigade. It was such a shame, not to mention how embarrassing that event was for all and sundry concerned. And one can scarcely imagine how small poor ol' Wee Willie must have felt.

After he was dramatically rescued, he proclaimed that he was never ever going to use his own bath anymore, just in case lightning struck twice and he ended up looking like a right berk again—a kind of 'once bitten, twice shy' kind of reasoning. I for one can fully understand why he should feel this way. Honestly. Being eventually hauled out of one's bath in the jacksy would be a totally unforgettable experience for anyone.

Consequently, he pledged to avoid this hazardous situation by using the nearby swimming baths instead.

'It was such a shame really. Life at times does tend to play cruel tricks. Realistically,' Grandma remarked after hearing about our neighbour's well-intentioned resolution, 'if Little Willie does pursue this course of action, he is in serious danger of being mistaken at the swimming pool for a . . . eh! . . . beached whale!'

Chapter Ten

I had the strangest incident the other day. It was so odd that I am almost hesitant to tell you about it. But I will, because I feel it will make you laugh. It's so important. And if you can have 'the craic' now and again, then life is so very worthwhile. It concerned, believe it or not, a lucky heather woman—you know the kind of person that's always popping up around the streets. I am sure you have noticed such folk. They always seem to have the appearance of a gypsy.

'Lucky heather, love?' A stocky elderly woman with a brown leathery face and a fading flowery dress approached me.

'I would love to . . . but I'm a bit skint,' I replied. Unfortunately, it was the same old story, I know, but it was true (as usual).

'Oh, go on! Give a *little* something. It can bring you such luck! Oh, go on . . .'

At that moment, I felt something in my pocket; it was two small objects. They weren't coins, but they were small and rounded. Aye, it turned out to be two wee Smarties. I had forgotten to eat them from about three days ago. However, all was not lost . . . whereupon I hit upon an excellent idea, a brainwave. It was simply this—to donate them as a generous gift to this 'travelling' lady, who, I was more than absolutely certain, would be more than pleased to receive them.

'There you go! I hope you enjoy them.' I put them gleefully in her hand and wished her all the best. I thought I had handled this very well. Tact or diplomacy was a great skill to develop, so Grandpa would always be pointing out. However, you would never guess in a thousand years what this woman would do next. Never! She didn't hand me my lucky heather or, come to think of it, even put some on the lapel of my school blazer. No indeed, what she did begin to do was, well, rather . . . eh! . . .

how can I say? . . . a bit shocking. Before I had time to receive her expected gratitude, she immediately proceeded to shove the lucky heather right up my 'conk'! Yes, right up my left nostril, to be precise. Now, how *unlucky* was that for starters?

She stormed off, muttering something under her breath about 'wayward youngsters' and 'bringing back National Service'. Crikey! I was now in the meantime almost suffocating from the after-effects of 'lucky heather syndrome'. Yet, she, 'the lady of the roads and highways', wasn't even in the least bit concerned at my unpleasant plight. No, not in the slightest.

Dramatically, I had no alternative in these circumstances, than to make an emergency visit to my local GP after this quite sudden and unexpected trauma. I can only try to communicate to everyone how a poor young Irish lad, totally defenceless and utterly exposed, felt in these all too real and perilous circumstances. Truly, I was feeling not only badly shaken but, to put it mildly, quite thoroughly stirred.

Disappointingly, and to be absolutely honest on this occasion, Doctor Petty wasn't much help either. Unforgivably, I didn't feel much sympathy coming from her for my plight. No, I certainly didn't. Definitely not—apart from the fact that she thankfully removed all the traces of lucky heather from my assaulted person and advised me in a rather obvious and predictable manner to steer clear of all lucky heather vendors, not only now but in the foreseeable future.

My local church at St Mary's of the Angels based in Moorehouse Road is very much part of my life. I go there every week, and the altars, the statues, the pulpit, and the pungent smell of the incense have seemed to lodge in my brain. The priests and the altar lads are very much part of the ceremony. (I am on the waiting list for being an altar boy as well being in the choir. It's been six years now.)

Apart from the lovely architecture and the beautiful religious paintings, the stained-glass windows always fascinated me with their extraordinary bright and shining colours. There was a harmony within. 'In the House of the Lord I will dwell . . .' Sister Magdalene, the nun who was always so encouraging and kind to me, would often quote this verse from the Good Book in my Bible-study class.

I went to the London Oratory School in Chelsea when I was eleven. It was so far removed from my primary school in Latymer Road. The latter looked like it was due for demolition, and bulldozers were getting ready to knock it down at any given moment. Nevertheless, apart from this, the teachers at St Francis Primary School were great and devoted, especially as there were sometimes thirty-five or more of us crammed into a tiny classroom. I am not sure how they, the staff, coped. It was no exaggeration to say that we 'little urchins' could be 'a right handful' to look after on many occasions.

The Oratory was located in a street called Stewart's Grove, a quiet residential back street. The building looked quite old, but it was kept in a good condition. There were two playgrounds. The first was for the first-year pupils, a sort of introduction to the school. The second was for all the other older pupils. I always remember the red creeping ivy on one of the main walls, which always struck me as being so charming. Nevertheless, the biggest difference was on a completely different level. The Oratory was a *mixed* school.

My street, as well as my neighbourhood, was my own personal domain where I dwelt. I got used to it because I really didn't have anything to compare it with. Deep inside my mind, I changed the recreational area at the rear of our flat, the Back, into a beautiful garden, as well as a well-equipped play area. It has everything my little heart could desire. Phew! There are so many things to do. I find that I have to pace myself. Life is a journey, and I am aware that I am most privileged to be here. By realising this, my existence becomes much more fulfilled and positive in so many different and fascinating ways.

I got a morning paper-round in Edgware Road in West London when I was twelve. The 'dosh' came in real handy. There was one problem though. This was that I was unable to get to school on time. After completing my paper round and returning home, I had to get changed into my school uniform and get two buses—one to High Street, Kensington, and a further one to South Kensington.

After a few weeks, my form master Mr Harper said he had had enough of me arriving late and was going to do something about it. Consequently, he gave me three strokes of the cane on my bum. Yikes! This hurt me like flamin' hell! He was the rowing master at the school and had a whacking arm that gave what can only be described as an 'out-of-body experience'.

Mr Carter, my English master, is just as bad and from the same mould. He gave me an equally good walloping a few weeks later, when he sent me out of his class for talking during his lesson. Do you know what? I'll be glad when the cane is banned. Until then, I'll have to make one hell of a grand effort to really, really behave myself.

I've always had my doubts about 'whackers' though. Yes, I have, especially those who often ask their victim during the ordeal such daft things as, 'Have I given you enough, boy?' or just as bad, 'Would you like me to dish out more of the same punishment with the cane to you, lad?' I for one would be certainly finding this topic quite funny if it wasn't *so* serious.

I've come to the astounding conclusion, and this may I say after much deep thought and reflection? Well, my findings are these—that such disciplinarian people probably study and practise for many years in their chosen profession to obtain what should be called a 'Medieval Torturer's Diploma'. And in Mr Carter and Mr Harper's case, they most surely would have passed without a shadow of a doubt with flying colours—'honours', to be sure.

No matter how hard I try, I just cannot get rid of my nickname 'Kilty-boy.' Even now complete strangers, actually come up to me in the street while taking a bit of exercise and ask me when I am making a comeback. A comeback, I ask you! The *Paddington Star*, our local rag, recently even had a few photos of me at Porchester on that very 'special' occasion under the caption, 'Will we ever laugh like this ever again?'

Both pictures showed me after my kilt had fallen unceremoniously down to the floor. Not funny! Even Mr Carter, who unbelievably was in the audience that eventful evening, every now and again reminds me with a bit of a corny remark, such as, 'I think it's about time, as you have been misbehaving again, that I warmed up naughty Kilty-boy's posterior!' He missed out on his calling and should have been a professional comedian instead. I think *not!*

It's the weirdest thing that everybody seems to run a mile and back at the mere mention of the word 'sex'. At the slightest mention of the word, Ma looks at myself as if I have just gone stir-crazy. Grandma, for her part, when the subject is raised, ends up giving me passages of the Bible to read. At least my sister Rita isn't so full on. She said she would get me a book that would explain 'everything'. Everything!

Michael, learning of my plight when he returned from holidays from university, loaned me a book on the subject called *The Road to Maturity*. It was very interesting. I hope that I manage to get on that particular road—one of these days.

I got to daydreaming the other day, and I am wondering if I need to see the doctor, because the person I was thinking about was none other than Mr Carter. Yes, and you will never guess what I was pondering on. I suspected Mr Carter of desiring to be an actor. I came to this surprising conclusion after I noticed he was always so keen on reading prose and poetry out loud. Shakespeare, Chaucer, and Dylan Thomas were among some of the distinguished literary folk that he often quoted.

However, and I know this might sound a bit peculiar or somewhat scary, I actually visualised Mr Carter being on stage as a look-a-like for none other than the famous actor and playwright of bygone years, Noel Coward himself! After much intellectual thought and painful research on my part, I surmised that 'Noel's' propensity for treading the boards would definitely be more interesting and far more exciting to him than teaching spotty and unappreciative nerds like me and my schoolmates. Aye, 'Mr Coward', like many other poor sods before him, after teaching countless young 'dimwits' down through the years, wished that he had really taken the bold step of treading the boards and had become a thespian instead.

'Patience is a virtue,' Ma would quote, when I told her I was a bit down and a wee bit anxious after not getting into the first-year school soccer team. Nevertheless, when I was at last selected in the second year, it was for me (I am sure you have noticed my enthusiasm) well worth the wait.

'Kicking the leather', as Gran always referred to it, was really, after all is said and done, great fun and wicked exercise. However, I hope that I am not stating the bleedin' obvious, but I must point out nonetheless that it is really a bit of a trial playing in mini-shorts in midwinter, wearing nothing more than a paper-thin T-shirt. Don't ask me why, but at this time of the year the weather always appear to plummet to record sub-zero temperatures. Truthfully, there was many an occasion when I couldn't even feel my fingers and toes, as well as other parts of my anatomy. Strange, but true!

We were having a long-distance run around the sports field at Barn Elms. Mr Jenkins, our sports master, instructed us sports enthusiasts that we had to run around it twice. This would have made it about a mile and a half distance. Eugene Murphy, our best runner, was not taking part owing to the fact that he had an irritating cold. I myself wasn't too bad at long-distance running; it probably had something to do with being a pal of Billy 'Jonah' Brankin.

In the race, I was well placed after a mile and a quarter—second, in fact. Cruising nicely along about ten yards behind my classmate Mick Mullins, I had made up my mind that I was intending to finish like a greyhound with a devastating burst of lightning speed. Mick was the school football team's star striker—a bit of a boaster, the 'bee's knees', and a bighead to boot. This was my perfect opportunity to get one over on him. Right on!

However, the fates were not kind to me at all. No, not at all on this occasion, as bleedin' adversity struck. Horror of horrors—would you 'Adam-and-Eve' it?—right out of the flamin' blue, I was suddenly zapped by the worst bloomin' stitch you could have possibly imagined in your entire life. I fell to the ground like a capsized flagpole. Arrrgh! The pain!

And what made things ten times flamin' worse was that as I lay recovering on the hard cold floor, I could see Mick Mullins galloping in like a bleedin' champion racehorse and pass the bloomin' finishing line punching the air in triumph. Yikes! Life at times can appear to be so unfair.

To makes matters worse, all the other lads simply continued to canter casually by and just looked at me strangely as I lay in agony on the floor. Don't ask me why! It was as if I had just grown two heads or something. Incredibly, not one of them even lifted a finger or as much as offered me a helping hand.

Eventually, after what felt like an eternity, one of the ground staff, whose mind seemed to be on something else (probably his girlfriend), spotted my tragic plight. He casually sauntered over to me and threw me over his shoulder without as much as saying a word, before depositing me like a sack of spuds in the changing rooms. Charming!

Billy and I felt that we needed cheering up, so we went to the Lofty Lion pub to hear a new comedian, Luke Lofthouse. We stood near the front door so we could hear properly. He was another new, young, up-and-coming comedian plying his trade.

A German couple were staying in a hotel in a lovely spot in Galway Bay. Sadly, although they were surrounded by such natural beauty, they were constantly at each other's throats like cats and dogs. This went on for quite a period of time, much to the dismay of other holiday-makers there, as well as the local people residing in the area. Eventually after about a week, the couple got into their car, and the man, who was driving, began to drive at full speed until their vehicle rocketed towards a cliff. However, when the car was just about to go over the cliff edge, the husband jumped out to save himself. However, the car went over the cliff, and his wife sadly perished. There was uproar in the area, and the German man was hauled before the local magistrate who asked him for a full explanation. The German man said it was simple really: his wife 'drove him to it!'

I said to Billy that Uncle Paddy had told me the Germans never ever had a sense of humour.

Chapter Eleven

At the Oratory a new girl has just joined. Her name is Jennifer Jackson. I missed her when she first arrived, as I was off from school for a few days owing to the fact that I dived into the local swimming pool and proceeded to hit my head on the bottom. Ouch! I forgot to put my hands out, which is quite important—as you would realise when diving. Everything went dark for about half a minute, but after that I think I made a full recovery.

Anyway, I heard she was a corker! However, I wasn't absolutely sure about girls, especially after my poor record with them over the years. Aye, I decided to walk warily as these past experiences with the opposite sex were still fresh in my memory bank.

Nonetheless, nothing could be further from my mind as I was sitting 'on the throne' in the boys' school toilet, engrossed in studying the Football League fixture list for the forthcoming season. Suddenly and without a word of warning, the toilet door was flung open, and standing there as bright as a new minted penny was none other than Jennifer herself.

'Oh sorry, I thought this was the girls'.' How odd! Jennifer seemed to be completely unaware that if it hadn't been for the strategic placement of my Football League fixtures, I could have been arrested by the local police for you know what!

'Well, it does say "boys" on the outside, you know . . .' I didn't wish to sound mean, but this was a bit much.

'So it does. I must have missed that. But why, by the way, is the cubicle unlocked? Not to worry. My name is Jennifer.' The reason why the locks were 'dodgy' was because some of the first-year boys had nothing better to do than to go round breaking toilet locks. Some people!

'Anyway . . .' I was going to stand up but remembered. 'This is not the best time for introductions.' As I said, I might have sounded a bit peeved, but there are times when we all need our privacy.

'Sure!' she smiled. 'I will look forward to making your acquaintance on another occasion.' She left, and all the rest of the day for some unexplainable reason I could smell a sweet fragrance fill the air.

In my dreams one of the things that I always fantasised about was being in the movies. Well, it certainly helps me to pass the time. And if not actually in the movie, at least photographing the big movie stars. Why not!? And, amazingly, I actually came *so* close with the latter dream. It just goes to show you that we never know what lies behind the next bend. Let me explain.

Our area was being used for making working-class and 'atmospheric' flicks. A few that come to mind are *Alfie* and *The L-Shaped Room*. A star whom I will never forget filming around our area was Judy Geeson. My brother saw her strolling down our street one day and had decided he just had to have some pictures of her. I guess he was a little shy because he asked me to do it. I thought, 'Why not . . . ?'

As I dashed off with his fully-loaded camera, I was dreaming of Hollywood and imagining how this could be the start of a wonderful career in show business. I caught up with Miss Geeson just as she was about to get into her car. She was gorgeous with her long blonde hair, flawless skin, blue eyes, and a fantastic smile.

She was so agreeable when I asked her to pose for me. She sat on the bonnet at the side of the car and also looked sensational sitting at the steering wheel. All the time, I was clicking away like a true professional. Puzzlingly, I could hear my brother way off in the distance shouting all kinds of things, but I couldn't make out what he was saying.

At the end of 'the photographic shoot' I wholeheartedly thanked Judy before she drove off with a heavenly smile on her face. I returned home, but not to a hero's welcome. No, not at all! Not on your nelly. It was only to find out the terrible news that all the shouting and hollering from my brother had been to remind me that I needed to roll the film on after each take. This I had forgotten to do.

Hence, the cold harsh truth was that none of my brilliant pics ever saw the light of day! 'Fools rush in!' Ma had no sympathy for Michael. No, none at all, and she said it served him 'blessed well right'. And instead of sending his wee younger brother, he should have 'got off his backside' and taken the trouble to take the photos himself.

I have climbed onto the roof to watch the 'goings on' go on . . . and on. I can hear the beautiful strains of various types of music from a Ceilidh band, remnants of jazz, folk, classical, and pop music. There is an unaccountable calm, and it makes me feel so peaceful and so relaxed. The time feels as if it is timeless.

Way up here, it is truly is remarkable how each and every single thing seems to settle down into a kind of sea of tranquillity. The feeling is out of this world and wonderful.

Meanwhile, I am feeling at ease with myself, and that is when the world is my very own exquisite oyster. Soon I encounter a white pigeon that appears out of nowhere—a fine-looking specimen of a bird, may I say? Extraordinarily, he appears to look at me strangely as if he has some kind of problem with myself. Me? Surely not! Nevertheless, in this standoff for several minutes my feathered friend continues to eye me up and down, seeming to indicate and proclaim in no uncertain manner, 'Up here, mate! It's only the birds who hang out on the roof.' Blessed cheek—some birds!

Unfortunately, there have been some skirmishes and fisticuffs between various black and white people around the Notting Hill area the other day. This is so very sad. Ma and Grandma and almost everyone else pray that these folk will see sense and make an effort to live together. I firmly believe that everything will all come right one day for sure, sometime, somewhere, in the not too distant future.

'Peace and Love.' Jeremiah, my musician buddy, says again with a conviction in his voice. 'A Higher Source will sort everything out one sweet day.' I know that he is another great one for getting down on his knees and praying his heart out. In the meanwhile, he skilfully plays a melodious tune on his guitar to a small gathering of folk. Again, I feel a sense of peace emanating from Jeremiah. And as he begins to sing he almost closes his eyes as he looks to the heavens.

Mr Carrol is a carpenter and an elderly resident of the Gardens. He produces lovely pieces of furniture, including chairs, beds, and wardrobes, which are all on display for everyone to see in the front room of his basement flat. Well, you might be surprised to be informed that he has only one arm, which makes his skill and endeavour even more remarkable. I personally think 'the showroom' is a great idea, because it shows all kinds of folk from 'outside' that although it's a bit rough and ready here, we still do have standards in our particular neck of the woods.

Billy, with his usually brashness, said that Mr Carrol, even with his disability, nevertheless, was a still a very *handy* person to have around the house. (I don't think so, Billy!) I couldn't possibly repeat what Mr Carrol threatened to do to Billy with his good arm after he was told of this remark concerning himself. 'He won't be such a clown after that. I can tell you that for nowt!' I don't think Mr Carrol thought that my mate Billy was much of a comedian after all.

Life around our place became one great big party when Uncle Jake suddenly announced he had hit the jackpot and won the football pools. All the relatives, friends, and neighbours sent their regards. I even took up playing the 'air guitar' right in front of the living-room mirror whilst singing my little heart out in celebration of his good fortune. (Eric Clapton, eat your heart out!) Jake even jacked in his job as a builder. He said the building site where he worked was making him ancient before his time. Apparently, without a moment's delay he also, informed the overbearing foreman in vivid and in no uncertain terms what he could do with his 'crummy' job.

Unfortunately, this story does not have a happy ending—quite the reverse, actually, a terrible one in fact. After a short while, much to his and everyone else's dismay, Uncle Jake made the awful and heart-stopping discovery that he had forgotten to post his football pools. 'It's amazing how someone can be penniless one day, a millionaire the next, but the following day go back to being skint. The eejit!' Auntie Flo, his wife, after being informed about the unsent coupon, was not in a generous or indeed (come to think about it) a very good or forgiving mood.

'Look before you leap!' Uncle Tommy suggested that this would be an appropriate quote for this particular occasion, especially as Uncle Jake's hobby was fishing. He often got away from it all by casting his rod in the Grand Union Canal that winds through our neighbourhood. However, I hope this doesn't mean in the present circumstances that Auntie Flo expects Uncle Jake, her husband, to leap into the Canal head first!

Chapter Twelve

Billy and I were feeling a bit bored, so we went to the Creepy Caterpillar pub to cheer ourselves up. 'Lanky' Larry Logan, a comedian from Dublin, was in full flow.

I was passing through a cemetery in Cork the other week, when I saw a poor soul kneeling down and pouring his heart out at a grave.

'Oh, my darling! My darling, why after all this time did you have to leave me? Why?'

Well, being a good Christian I just couldn't just walk on by, so I approached the sorrowing man to say, 'My good fellow, I can see how upset you are. You must have really loved your wife?'

He looked up at me with a strange look in his eye before answering.

'What are you talking about? My wife is well and at home making my tea. This is my girlfriend!'

Billy fell on the floor laughing his head off. My brother was just the same. He bought a joke book, and every time he told a joke from it, he roared out laughing. I laughed too—not that I always got the joke. It is just that the sight of Michael rolling about in hysterics always made me laugh too.

I am beginning to explore the area that surrounds the Oratory in Chelsea. The King's Road is always buzzing with excitement, and as it is so near, I often stroll up and down it during the lunch hour. If I have a bit more time, I like to stroll down to the Chelsea Barracks where the smart Chelsea Pensioners reside. Also, it's nice to amble down to the Thames Embankment and watch the river flow. It is wonderful to be able to get away from the crowd and let one's hair down

I've just had another read of that great little piece of writing called *The Little Prince*. What a splendid read! It may be even better the second time round. He lived alone on a tiny planet no larger than a house. He owned a unique flower—one of great beauty. He started to wander and came to the Earth, where he learned from a fox what is really important in life. The truth is, 'There is so much more to life than we could ever possibly imagine.' That's so cool.

Do you know that everything seems to be different when the Beatles are singing 'All You Need Is Love', not to mention all their other great songs? But the former has always remained truly one of my favourites. Aye, It will be so great and so unifying when everyone eventually sings it together—aye, supernaturally and breathtakingly, 'All You Need Is Love'!

I've always noticed that when Ma is playing bingo and the numbers are not going her way, she cries out expectantly to the bingo-caller, 'Stir 'em up!' I think she means to stir her numbers up so things will go well for her in the game. Do you know that I can identify with that? I also need my numbers stirred up every now and again so that things will go well for myself, for sure and without a shadow of a doubt.

'Stir 'em up!'

I decided against my better judgement to accept Jennifer's invitation to her 'masked ball'. As usual, there was only one small snag; I didn't have a mask. Jennifer told me not to worry, as she had one that would suit me down to a tee. I trusted her implicitly. Tantalisingly, when I arrived at the masked ball there were about twelve guests already there. About half of them were some friends from school, and the other half were relatives and some local friends. Her parents were, thankfully, nowhere to be seen. Grown - ups *do* sometimes spoil the fun for us young'uns by getting in the way.

Masks included Supergirl, Wonder Woman, Batman and Robin, Superman, and Spiderman. In my opinion, I thought Jennifer's mask looked great. It was a Venetian mask, apparently originating in Venice many years ago where people liked to be daring. It was important in their lives back then to really have fun. Jennifer's mask was all golden bright and 'silvery-sparkly', but at the same time mysterious and exotic. It summed her up beautifully, and without wishing to appear a wee bit biased, I thought she looked like total and utter perfection.

I was the last guest to arrive at Jennifer's do. I suppose it was a case of myself being somewhat theatrical. I am referring to the fact that I liked to make a grand entrance on such occasions. By this time, everyone was gathered together in Jennifer's living room. To me it looked like a room from Buckingham Palace. Sensationally, there was a huge chandelier in the midst of this room that seemed to contain a million-and-one lights. The furnishings were superb and pricey, and there was no sign of a metal bath (like my family had) in front of the marble fireplace. I couldn't see any coal or, come to think of it, even a coal bucket. Maybe, I thought, they had hidden it.

After introducing me quickly to her guests, she ushered me into another beautifully furnished guest room, which was situated at the back of the living room. She seemed excited as she was informing me that she had saved a 'brilliant' mask just for me. I must admit now that I did get a bit of a shock when I was presented with it by Jennifer herself. It can only be described as what I would call a . . . eh! . . . *rather* different mask.

Guess what? I am trying to be very fair here—aye, I am—but my good self was expecting something a little more . . . well . . . eh . . . suave or—how should I put it?—something a bit more sophisticated. Well, to put it bluntly, it was flamin' neither. May I add also that my enthusiasm to attend this gathering was now well and truly eliminated when the mask Jennifer produced for me was nothing other than a chimpanzee that was sporting a pair of horn-rimmed glasses. Cor blimey! And if this wasn't bad enough, there was a huge banana drooping down from his mouth. Don't ask me why. Maybe it was because he was feeling a bit hungry.

'Jennifer, is this some kind of joke?' I asked.

'No, not at all. It's a mask that could be used in a new Hollywood movie. It could be a monster, monster hit, so Pops says.' I forgot to mention that 'Pops,' her dad, was a film-director. (And I bet Jennifer didn't have to save up for a month like me to go to the cinema either.)

'I think you should send him back to the jungle.'

'But he's not real.'

'I know. I was only joking.'

'Please, put it on, just for me.'

I don't know what it is about lovely and beautiful girls, but when they ask me for anything and they fix me with their loving and tender looks, I am a complete goner. Sorry to say, I wasn't always like this, but I am now.

'Okay, okay, never let it be said that I don't like to have a sense of humour.' Whereupon I put on the mask. His name was Charlie by the way, and I felt like a proper Charlie, I can tell you for nothing.

I went back to the living room with Jennifer. She asked me to wait outside the room and to enter only when she introduced me. When she did so, there was an odd hush from everyone. This was followed by an erupting ripple of laughter that culminated in her boyfriend doing an awful Elvis impersonation.

'Ever thought of visiting Memphis, Tennessee, daddy-o, so you can get up to any monkey business you like? Thank you so very much!'

What a blessed and champion eejit! Ugh!! I felt sick.

Needless to say, this was my first masked ball, and it would in all likelihood be my absolute last. I have never liked Elvis impersonators at the best of times. Yet, even now when I was barely a teenager, I already had one too many versions of 'Heartbreak Hotel', and I never wanted to own a pair of 'Blue Suede Shoes'.

Chapter Thirteen

I had this spectacular dream the other night. I was on this ship, a kind of galleon, a very strong and stately ship. I was at the helm, steering magnificently through the towering waves as cool as a cucumber. Suddenly and quite unexpectedly, the waves became overpowering, but instead of my ship submerging into the depths of the sea, it began to elevate and stay suspended beneath a sky that was full up with huge staring eyes.

I've decided to go to the Paddington recreational ground where they have a have a running track. I like to run and run there, knowing all the time that my strength and stamina are increasing. Somehow it helps to clear my head. (I am still attempting to apply Dr Petty's advice 'to remain cool, calm and collected'.) Although I feel quite exhausted after my exertions at the track, there is nothing quite like a long refreshing shower to make me feel quite grand again. Whew! There is nothing quite like a bit of exercise to get myself in tune. I can almost feel my blood pumping around my body on full speed, mind you. I am for sure walking and running myself to health.

Ma says that when she works at cleaning the sauna, the sweat is pouring off her. I think I can say that after my efforts at the running track, I can only imagine in a small way and appreciate what she means. Her shopping bags seem to be getting bigger and bigger as her family continues to grow. I must repeat once more how much I really appreciate all the love and all the sacrifices that she has constantly made down through the years as she traipses around the streets of Paddington on behalf of us all. And because of her, the roads, byways, and walls don't appear to be so worn out, dirty, and smoke-blackened.

For my good deed of the week, I decided to visit Kitty O' Hanlon, an elderly Irish widow who lived by herself around the corner in Ledbury

Road. Her house had now been condemned, and she was very anxiously waiting to be rehoused by the Council.

'If you're going to do something, whatever it may be, make a darn good job of it.' This is not only Grandpa's philosophy but Grandma's, Ma's, Pa's and almost everyone else's point of view in my family circle, including myself too.

'She's a lovely person, but very small, thin, and haggard. It is such a pity,' Grandpa stated. 'In all my days, I've never seen an ol' biddy that is such an awful bag of nerves.'

Upon arriving at the 'shack', I was greeted warmly by a very worried-looking Kitty. In this big and lonely house, almost every possible sound seemed to cause Kitty to jump out of her skin. I thought I was a bit on the 'nervy' side myself, but she really took the biscuit. I thought to myself, 'Not to worry, though, as it takes all sorts to make up this great big world that we all inhabit, doesn't it?'

Anyway, upon my arrival Kitty was hospitable enough to make me a lovely cup of tea (with a jam doughnut), and we were having a right ol' chinwag. I can't tell you everything she said, as I was hearing some rather colourful and interesting gossip. I think the term used has something to do with 'blue'. I promised her I wouldn't repeat what she told me, and a promise is a promise. Aye, I think she was, as they say, 'letting it all hang out'.

To be perfectly honest, it had crossed my mind earlier that evening that my visit might be a wee bit boring or, to say the least, not too interesting for myself, but as I have already mentioned, this was far from the case.

Incredibly, she had a very varied and interesting life, albeit a tough one with many ups and downs, as she recalled her life in Ireland as well as here in England. Do you know what? I made the startling revelation that we all can learn so much if we only stop, look, and listen. Aye.

Anyway, getting back to Kitty, she had for sure lived most of her days in another lifetime. As we whiled the hours away, I was intrigued by the many weird and wonderful tales that she was able to relay to myself. For sure, some episodes in her life made me really laugh, while others—well, to be absolutely even-handed—brought a tear to my eye.

Dear ol' Kitty was a natural storyteller, and it was very touching and so evident how devoted she still was to her departed husband, whom she would refer to every now and again. To top it all, Kitty herself knew absolutely everything about, well, everyone, as well as every single event that was of any consequence in the neighbourhood. Straight up! We were having what one might call as 'a right ol' grand get-together.'

I was so pleased, because I observed that Kitty was now visibly relaxing. Extraordinary! After some time we were getting on splendidly and—dare I say in view of what was to eventually materialise later—'like a house on fire'.

Our pleasant and most interesting time together was interrupted by a sudden strange popping sound. It took both of us several minutes to discover what the source of this was. It turned out after some diligent investigation to be a light bulb that had inconveniently fused in her living room. After this happened, both Kitty and I were sitting in splendid isolation right there in her living room almost invisible.

All of a sudden, Kitty became very upset and agitated and asked me if I could be so kind as to change the light bulb. I responded by saying of course, no problem. She then kindly advised me to turn the power off at the mains, which I did, before inserting the new bulb. Afterwards, I went back to turn the power on at the mains. It should have been a simple procedure, but it was not.

As soon as I flicked the light switch on, flaming sparks began to appear everywhere with alarming regularity. It was like bonfire night with the fireworks and all, but neither of us was enjoying the spectacular show. In the meantime, the light bulb flickered on and off for a short period of time before it ceased, along with the fantastic 'firework display'—thankfully! However, by this time, Kitty was shaking uncontrollably like a leaf in a hurricane, and she and I were like two lone figures, resembling Tweedledum and Tweedledee, standing there in the complete and utter darkness.

What made things even much worse at this point was the fact that poor ol' Kitty now began to scream and holler so much so that if anyone had happened to be passing at the time, they might have come to the conclusion that she was being murdered by myself. And I am too young for prison.

I told her not to worry. I would go and get some help. In the meantime, I managed by some miracle to carefully steer my way out of this bleak house. She wasn't the only one feeling somewhat flustered. Skilfully, I managed to navigate myself home with great athleticism and precision. Then I immediately told Pa what had happened. He, like a bat out of hell, rang the emergency line for the Westminster City Council, who got a qualified bloke around to fix 'freakin' out' Kitty's electrics.

After the chaos had eventually died down and the dust had finally settled, Pa said that he was now definitely cancelling my enrolment in the Junior Electricians' Apprenticeship Course!

At the Oratory we had a Scottish headmaster by the name of Mr Gadfly. He was a good headmaster, but he was always so austere and looked so dreadfully serious. His face always reminded me of a constipated barn owl. He stood so upright, as if he was some kind of general in the army and we poor 'recruits' were his very own soldiers.

Annoyingly, he had a rather irksome habit of repeating at the end of each sentence the words 'just noo!' I think what he meant to say was 'just now'. I really didn't have the nerve or courage to ask him whether his phrase was 'just noo' (the Scottish equivalent meaning of 'just now'). Sincerely, I had just recently learnt at this stage in my young life that there is a time to speak and an apt time to shut up or to 'zip it up'! I instinctively opted for the latter.

Now, I am not one to hold a grudge, and I will go as far as to profess that I do hold to the noble desire to 'let bygones be bygones.' In fact, 'live and let live' has always been the motto that I have sincerely tried to live by—a kind of schoolboy code, if you like. But what happened the other day did literally make my blood boil. This unfortunate incident caused the blood to rise right up to the top of my head like a raging storm—and at any given moment it was in danger of spilling right over.

Let me explain the reason for this chagrin. Since I had been suffering from a wee bit of a dodgy chest lately, Ma had the brilliant idea of knitting me a bigger version of the Oratory slipover—a much bigger version. True, it was about five times larger than the original, but Ma did keep faithfully to the same colour and design. I loved it. It certainly was nice and chunky and very warm. To sum up concisely how I felt, it was just what the doctor ordered to keep the chilly-willy, cold weather at bay.

Anyway, it was in the early winter morning after Assembly when my classmates and I were parading or, rather, shuffling by the Headmaster's office under the ever-watchful eye of 'General' Gadfly himself. I would like to point out that everything up to now was going hunky-dory and right on song that particular day—until I was spotted by the 'eagle eye' of Mr Gadfly.

Sincerely, I am telling you no word of a lie. He swept down on me like some kind of prehistoric T. Rex, whilst waspishly muttering, 'What have I here . . . just noo?' Before I could even say 'Arsenal for the Cup', he started to pull my 'designer' slipover right off my person. And if this wasn't bad enough, it didn't even seem to occur to 'General' Gadfly that it might have possibly been a very good idea to remove my school jacket before doing so.

Sensationally, by the time it did occur to him, my slipover by now was totally wrapped halfway around my neck so much so that I could have almost died of suffocation.

The trials and tribulations of a young life . . .

Chapter Fourteen

I told Billy a joke recently. It went as follows.

> At the bottom of the sea-bed, a cod met a prawn and made a
> pass by saying, 'Your *plaice* or mine?'

Billy for once didn't laugh, but I did. I don't know why, but I couldn't
help myself for some minutes. I didn't actually fall on the floor with
laughter, but I nearly did. It is so true: there is nothing quite like having a
good ol' belly laugh. P-l-e-a-s-e try it!

I was so chuffed recently that I was awarded the prize at school for
English Composition. It was a book entitled *A Visit to the Holy Land*. I
was really over the moon about this, because it was the very first time I had
ever been awarded a prize at school. When I told Ma, she was immediately
ecstatic and got down on her hands and knees and said a prayer of thanks
to the heavens above. Afterwards, she made me a cup of sweet 'tae', and
proceeded to tell all and sundry in the neighbourhood about my good
news. I think she was more pleased than I was about this.

The prize I was given was the loveliest book that I had ever seen
in my entire life. It was beautifully illustrated, and the text was very so
informative and interesting. Everything about this captivating book was
enthralling and clear. Added to this, it proved to be a real boon and aid
in my Bible-study class. Sister Magdalene herself was so pleased about
my prize that she unexpectedly informed the whole class about my good
fortune.

Whoopee! And it was the cherry right on top of the cake when she
even suggested that my prize might have even been a loving reward or an
indirect gift from none other than God Himself. (Thanks, God!)

My favourite photo was a picture of the Dome of the Rock situated in Jerusalem. This beautiful building has such grace and loveliness and is adorned with such splendid colours of green, turquoise, and gold. It is a truly wonderful and remarkable place, which always reminds me of Jerusalem. It had such religious significance and means such a lot to so many people—and rightfully so, because it is so unique and magnificent. I showed Ma my book and the beautiful text, photos, and illustrations. She was so pleased as well. She said that when she could save up enough money, she would take me to the Holy Land one day. You know what? It goes without saying that I will really look forward to that.

I suppose you know you are growing up when you see your siblings going out with their respective girlfriends and boyfriends. I am still waiting patiently for my turn 'stepping out' and 'hitting the tiles'. Is it now or never? In the meantime, I'll keep looking up to the wonderful sky to be constantly awestruck by the sheer splendour and o-m-n-i-p-r-e-s-e-n-c-e of it all.

We have a dog called Timmy. He is a white poodle, and we all love him. He loves us very much in return. We give him lots of nice things to eat and drink, and we give him plenty of exercise. One thing about Timmy that I observed is that when I take him out for 'walkies', he doesn't like in the least to be rushed. He's a funny ol' sausage really! He stops every few feet to sniff lampposts, pavements, and just about anything that moves, including humans as well as other dogs. If I have the flamin' cheek to rush him, he gives me such a look as if to say, 'Do you bleedin' well mind!'

'In the zone! In the zone! My boy, you have got to get into the blessed zone . . . and stay there!' Uncle Paddy was in an enthusiastic mood and kept on telling me that the world could be my oyster if only I wanted it to be.

And I was 'in the zone' on Saturday morning when I scored my thousandth goal around the Back. What a gem! I received the ball on the right wing, but I decided to drift into the centre of the pitch, where in one beautiful movement I beat two defenders and subtly slotted it into corner of the other team's net. What A G—O—A—L! Break out the champagne! However, fizzy lemonade will have to do on this occasion as I am too young to drink.

I had a wonderful dream the other day. A proper cracker! I dreamt that I was again a brilliant butterfly. Alas, I was not any old butterfly as I soared above the landscapes, the rivers, and the oceans. No, not in the least! I was a special butterfly. Aye, it was the most brilliant feeling as I felt myself drawn towards the captivating glow of the warm amber sun. I could remember from my book of butterflies that I was a monarch butterfly, and something deep in my soul told me loud and clear that this life had *no* hold on me.

Astronomically, with a deep breath and an all-encompassing sigh, I am strapping on once more my helmet and getting into my chariot. W-o-w-e-e-e-e-e! I think it is the appropriate time to shout 'Hallelujah! Hallelujah!! Hallelujah!!!' Again I am telling myself, 'Elijah, you are not the only one who can leave this earth and all its cares behind, and rise up once more into the Welcoming-Heavenly-Hallelujah-Heights!'

Chapter Fifteen

'It's all about timing.' Uncle Samuel was musing over a strong pint of stout in one of the local bars dotted around Paddington, West London. It was a typical wet afternoon that was all too familiar and synonymous with an English winter. 'It has a toucan as a symbol.' He gazed into a near empty glass as if it was a crystal ball. 'I suppose it means, when you are in the groove, you are in the blessed groove! What else in the name of the heavens could that daft looking toucan mean? What else?'

'Let me hold him. Let me love him. Let me hold this dear, precious child,' I recall my Grandma say to me shortly before she departed from us. 'Let me hold him and love him whilst I have this opportunity to do so.'

Myself, I have just turned seventeen years of age in what only be described as the time of my life. Yippee! Everyone says that, Kevin the garcoon is growing up, and I am. Nonetheless, everything that has happened is all in the past, and I am looking forward to the exciting and expectant future. Can I ask you a question though? Have you ever noticed that some folk seem to always live in the past? It's odd. It's as if they are somewhat fearful to take a positive step forward into what lies ahead of them. Have you? Well, I have. But enough about this startling and amazing observation. This is now the appropriate time to move on.

I've taken up oil painting as a hobby. I really love it. I am not much good at it at present, but I find it so relaxing, and it is so great to retreat into. I don't think that one has to be particularly good at something to get a great deal of pleasure out of that subject. It's definitely a case of each to his or her own.

'Do what you can while you have the time. We have so little precious time.' Melissa was in one of her moods. I'm in my blue period. Well, it's just that everything I paint seems to turn out blue. What? Should I see the shrink when I go into my pink period? Well, I only asked.

Enough of this frivolity! Nevertheless, allow me to enter straight away into something which is of some immediate importance in the present—straight to the heart of the matter for sure. Yours truly is well and truly hooked and completely infatuated by a girl in the sixth form. It will not come as the shock of the ages that I am referring to a girl whose name is Jennifer Jackson. Aye, I think you have cottoned on to this fact since she joined my school, the London Oratory, but I am still fighting the feeling. And what is that feeling, you may well ask yourself. The answer is, 'Will my affection for the lovely and gorgeous Jennifer ever be reciprocated?' Who really knows? Who cares, and who will ever flippin' well know? In the blessed meantime, under my umbrella of love so as to speak, I am walking solo.

I must admit that I not the best of students at school, and ploughing my way through my A levels is proving to be a one hell of a task. However, my life turns out to be a wee bit more tolerable when I play for the school football team. There's nothing quite like participating in a particular exercise that one really enjoys. Really, believe you me, it is of vital importance. It most definitely is. Personally, one of the massive benefits of doing this is that it gets my blood pumping big time around my wiry and skinny body. Problems and irritations tend to disappear, and fears and worries turn out to be *not* such a big deal after all.

Extraordinarily, and honestly to be sure, my school footie chums and I, we hardly ever win any of our soccer matches against other schools. No, hardly any at all! As a matter of fact, out of sheer desperation we've taken lately to filling out our own penalty area with our team during play. Yes, that is rather non-adventurous, I must admit. There is one exception: we leave a lone striker upfront, the reason being that we are looking and hoping for a sudden, lucky breakaway that might give us a surprise win. (It's only a game after all.)

I had another one of my dreams the other night. It was fantastic. I was up in the Himalayas looking down on the valleys and spectacular vistas from my beautifully carved out cave. My abode was sensationally decorated with candles and scented with joss sticks. I walked around this place that can only be described as having celestial overtones. The air felt like it was a delicate perfume, and the colours, sights and sounds were, well, out of this world! Somehow—how shall I put this?—everything felt as if it was just supernaturally peaceful.

Mind-bogglingly—and I can't put enough emphasis into this breaking and sensational news—last rainy and windy Saturday turned out to be such a wonderful and special day. The zenith! Of course, you are fully aware that I wouldn't dare to spin you a Gaelic yarn. No, not me. Now listen to my good self, because things are starting to get much better for me. Surprise of surprises, my school football team and I had an extremely rare and precious win, one-nil to be precise. I know what you are thinking. 'What great, wonderful and thrilling news!' I agree, but that wasn't the only significant thing that occurred. In addition, yours truly got the one and only goal. Yes, me! Isn't that absolutely brilliant?

I was played as the lone striker in this particular game, as our usual striker Mick Mullins was side-lined with a bad cold. His mother, who always faithfully supported us every week in and week out, blamed our team's poor football tactics for his illness. Hmm, strange, but she was right and absolutely correct that her son's ailment was down to him getting very little exercise during our school matches and, consequently, this led to him having 'his assets frozen off'. (Aye, she did have a certain way with words). I must be perfectly candid here and admit that the team tactics did mean that we hardly ever got the ball up the soccer pitch to poor ol' Mick.

However, 'every cloud has a silver lining' was one of Pa's very favourite sayings, and in this particular case it indeed proved to be spot on. Aye, precisely, right on the money. Okay, with hand on heart, it might have something to do with a wee bit of desperation in our team, and also, the simple fact that nobody else amongst our mob had the faintest inclination to fill Mick's shoes meant that I myself was unanimously selected to fill this role.

At this momentous time I can most modestly report that this will always remain a rare and treasured moment in my own sporting history. Most definitely! Even if I do say so myself, my winning goal was sheer poetry in motion.

Let me relate to you the scene and run through what happened. I coolly collected the ball in my own half of the field as it was hooved out by our beleaguered and rapidly tiring defence. I proceeded to dribble it down the field, before slotting it past a rather casual goalkeeper. (He was reading a newspaper at the time.)

Yes, 'Georgie Best' was the victorious hero who saved the day. Phew! I can still relish this moment. Oh, to be appreciated and lauded to boot! In my humble opinion there is nothing quite like a bit of lauding. A wee bit of encouragement can go a long, long way. It is so true. I am not too bashful to admit that I bathed, unashamedly, in a glow of thankfulness after the match for a good hour or two.

However, this euphoric feeling soon turned out to be a rather short-lived and whimsical experience. I will not beat around the bush; that is not my way. I am not sure how I should put it, but later on that day things turned out to be nothing short of horrendous.

I have already mentioned that on Saturday morning I was still floating on the wings of praise for my unexpected goal. Thus, there I was standing on Earl's Court Station, returning home and feeling so good, when who do you think I should accidentally bump into? Have you guessed it? No? Well, it was none other than Jennifer herself. Wow! I hardly recognised her. She was not in a daft school uniform like me, but dressed up to the nines with a black mini-skirt and a striking red blouse. Whew! It had a very low cleavage—so much so that I could almost see most of her you know what! But hey, I am no prude! Never!

It was like a electric bolt out of the proverbial blue. We greeted each other, but for some unknown reason I just couldn't take my eyes of her bosoms. Sad, I know. Mr Bartram, my biology teacher, professed it had something to do at this stage of my life with my hormones.

Anyhow, after I'd mainly recovered my composure, I asked her how she was, and she asked me the same. Suddenly and unexpectedly, this elderly dude—well to me he looked at least in his mid-twenties if not older—sailed up next to Jennifer and proceeded to place his arm around her waist.

'Hey, babe, is everything okay?' This dark, medium-sized, and vaguely good-looking geezer asked Jennifer—and, I may add, with a wee bit of suavity as well as intensity. It was as if he was her very own Romeo and she was his Juliet. How sad was that! I instinctively took a disliking to him. Don't ask me why, but if you were to press me, I would say that in my unbiased opinion I was none too impressed with his greased back hair, Armani suit, and Rolex watch—most definitely, in my fair opinion, a right bleedin' show off!

Jennifer introduced me to him and informed her new boyfriend that we both went to the same school. His name was Piers by the way. Well,

I didn't mind the name, but to be honest I found him a bit toffee-nosed as well as being located somewhere right up his own a***! (I'm sorry if I seem a bit coarse, but I have brought it up before; you know I like to call a spade a spade.)

Now you might consider that I was acting a little immature, but for my part and in my own defence, I had decided that this was probably a passing stage in Jennifer's development too. Therefore, in true Christian mode, I decided I would forgive her and let this incident pass. However, Piers then rudely asked, 'Sonny, how do you enjoy school life?'

'Sonny'! The blessed cheek of the man! I was seventeen and—without stating the bleedin' obvious—going on eighteen. This upstart of a yuppie was definitely pushing his luck to the extreme and beyond. And if it wasn't for the fact that I was still attending Bible-study classes and practising meditation in between, I would have most surely have given him one hell of a mighty left hook right up his arrogant bracket. Who could have blamed me? Henry Cooper, I can inform you that you would have been proud to have witnessed it! I am quite certain of this salient fact. I am only flesh and blood after all.

'There's so much to do but s-o-o-o-o little time to do it,' Melissa, Eileen's friend, suddenly proclaimed, when I reported her about what had occurred at Earl's Court. Do you know what? I don't wish to sound like a moaning old git, but Melissa—a lovely girl, I do admit—does have this annoying tendency to state on some occasions the bleedin' obvious.

Chapter Sixteen

It's another rainy, foggy, windy, and frosty day in London town. I believe I have, completely by chance, stumbled on a unique finding. Well, it is for me anyhow. This finding that I have excavated is that too many people, and not just the elderly, are becoming incontinent. Talk about bad odours! What could possibly, in the name of the heavens, be the real reason for this recent worldwide epidemic? (Answers on a postcard please, but only clean ones will be considered.)

I'm looking at another blank page. Yes, another stark-bare canvas. 'What's happening to my inspiration?' I ask myself. I've actually been sitting here for weeks, months, and what feels like bloomin' years, and nothing appears to be happening. There should be an organisation for artists called 'Writer's Block' with the subheading 'Get your pipes unblocked here!' Someone had to think of it.

'God is an Irishman!' Uncle Paddy is trying to convince the local church that he had what I think they refer to as a visitation. You know the type of thing I am referring to—a Lourdes or a Fatima type of experience. His 'visitation' was, I think, verging on a vision as well. He dreamt he was in Egypt on Mount Sinai where I believe God appeared to Moses. The startling difference was that Uncle Paddy announced to all and sundry that God suddenly appeared to him out a burning bush as well and announced, 'I am an Irishman!'

The amazing thing about all of this was that more than a few of the local people actually and incredibly believed him. Rumours were rife all over the neighbourhood until it was eventually discovered by his spouse that Uncle Paddy had drank two bottles of whisky as well as a bottle of brandy the very same night he had 'the vision'. This evidence was discovered stashed underneath his lumpy mattress. Pa said that if Uncle Paddy had drank any more, there was a distinct possibility he would have announced that his wife was, in reality, the Virgin Mary!

'There is no distance between you and me.' Melissa was in full flow, and why not? I asked her to forgive my wee bit of irritation a little earlier on in the week as she had caught me in a bad mood. She declared, however, she hadn't any recollection of this occasion. Yipes! And I thought I was the one with the bad memory.

'Get yourself a pet!' Ma was in a good mood. Timmy, our newly acquired white poodle, was lovely. 'If you're lonely and need the company and you desire someone to talk to, there's nothing finer. And they don't have the blessed cheek to answer you back as a lot of the naughty rascals do these days.' She paused to take a determined breath. 'The exercise will do you good and it will surely help, by Jesus, in trimming down your ever-widening waistline. Saints in the heavens above! We're turning into the devil's own nation of blessed fatties!'

'What a difference a day makes!' Billy Brankin, my mate, was worrying me because he was not being his normal devil-may-care self. I think he was having girl trouble, but unlike me he had a tendency to bottle things up. Sensitive people have a tendency to be a bit like this. It's true! It was either this or his latest scheme to blow up the London Oratory School was not going to plan. He was hoping against all hope that he could pull the latter off without anyone even noticing. However, it was just another one of his hare-brained schemes that was going the way of all flesh.

'He's going through the adolescent blues.' Grandpa was a gem when it came to being understanding. 'I was young once, so I know what he is going through.' He thought for a moment before continuing. 'Take him out somewhere and be a friend to him. Get his worrying mind off things.'

The only place I could think of to take Billy that was conveniently close and cheap was the Fat Hog. It fitted the criteria exactly: it was in the proximity and mercifully free. Now, I'm honestly putting my cards on the table here. This so called public house was so rough and ready that you could have been forgiven for thinking that some of the clientele who patronised the place were straight out of the saloons of the Wild West. It was even rumoured that Billy the Kid and Jesse James were born above this pub before they both decided to emigrate to the good ol' USA. I do admit, though, this was only a rumour.

Let's face it. Pubs must come up with new ideas to survive in a competitive industry these days. The Fat Hog, realising this down-to-earth fact, was advertising a forthcoming talent competition. Nevertheless, that particular evening there was a one-legged comedian called 'Hopalong Cassidy' appearing. He was supposed to be very funny, and let's be honest, with a name like that he was off to a great start.

I hope I am not sounding facetious or cruel, but when Hopalong appeared, I was taken aback by two things. No, as a matter of a fact I stand corrected. There were in fact three things. First, as this was supposed to be Cassidy's debut, I must confess that I was expecting someone a wee bit younger than a man of eighty-nine. Apparently, he carried his birth certificate as proof—as if anyone needed it! I thought to myself when I saw him that he looked older than Grandma and Grandpa combined.

Second, he was dressed as a zany character from a Western movie in a flamboyant white outfit with tassels and all, and he kept on repeating for no apparent reason 'Yeehaaa!' When Billy clapped eyes on Hopalong, he quipped that a more appropriate name for him would have been 'the Jurassic Cowboy'.

Third, I couldn't understand why he didn't simply use a crutch when he was on the stage. For me, seriously, I had the distinct impression that Hopalong was going to keel over at any given moment. It was (without wishing to sound silly) an act in the balance or a balancing act. Anyway, his performance began on a firm footing—at least to start off with.

> There was an Englishman, a Welshman, and an Irishman being held in a prison by a cruel dictator. Suddenly, after years of being incarcerated, the dictator came in unexpectedly to their cell and declared (because he was in a good mood) that if each of them could sing a song about a dog, he would immediately release them.

> Thereupon, the Englishman sang a lovely song about Lassie, and the dictator liked it so much that he said he was released. This was followed by the Welshman, who gave a lovely rendition of 'Old Shep' and was also granted his freedom. When it came to the Irishman, he started to sing 'Strangers in the night'! The dictator was a little confused about this and soon butted in.

'Hang on, hang on. I said I wanted you to sing a song with a dog in it!'

'Hold your horses, I haven't finished yet!' And he continued to sing '. . . Scooby dooby do . . .'!

Upon saying the delivery line, Hopalong unaccountably slipped right off the stage, and an ambulance was called to rush him to hospital. On the one hand it was a tragedy, as I was informed that it hastened Hopalong into early retirement from show business. What a shame! However, on the other hand, it did do the trick for my mate Billy. By a weird twist of fate, it caused him to revert back to his normal self - normal for him, anyway. Aye, how strange life can be! Apparently, and the proof is in the pudding, all of this was triggered by the unfortunate 'Jurassic Cowboy's' fall from grace.

Anyhow, with people like Hopalong regularly featuring at the Fat Hog, it will come as a surprise that there was a talent contest' in the flippin' first place!

Chapter Seventeen

'Boy, keep your knees up!' Mr Jenkins, the sports master, bellows out at myself as I am counting the miles on a cross-country run. 'I'll put you through your paces, Barry. Deep breathing will do the trick, my lad. It is either that, or you'll end up killing yourself.' How considerate.

'I would hate to be inside a volcano when it erupts!' Uncle Tommy, I found, always had such interesting thoughts. He was so amusing that Ma said that you wouldn't need a television if you lived with him—he was that entertaining. However, I think his wife, Auntie May, would still prefer the TV instead.

I am still absorbing the atmosphere of the Gardens and its surrounding area even after all these years. There are ice-cream vans ringing out the joy of tasty treats in a kind of rocking-chair rhythm that somehow stirs up the senses. Cars appear to honk for no apparent reason as usual. All of this is complemented by the Gaelic songs Ma remembers and sings, as they echo through the rooms and passageways of our dwelling. It's a lucid and a salient fact that sometimes there is a fine line between reality and dreaming.

In the meantime, the scent of jasmine and lotus blossom emanating from outside in the Back momentarily takes me back to the Himalayas.

There was a fracas above our place in the third-floor flat in the Gardens the other evening. However, it took a whole week to find out the real reason for this occurrence. Aye, it was a full week later when it was reported in the local paper the *Paddington Star*. What had happened was that the lady and her husband had a domestic fight, and whilst doing so he quite insanely pulled tufts of her hair from her scalp and obviously left her in a stressed-out state. She called the police, and her husband was duly arrested and taken to court for common assault. Consequently, it appeared under the arresting headline:

A HAIR-RAISING EXPERIENCE!

Billy and I felt that we were being starved of entertainment and were determined not to miss the talent show at the Fat Hog. However, to put this as inoffensively as possible, regarding the talent on show—well, there was precious little talent to be seen. Yes, it was such a shame! We didn't think it was humanly possible for the folk that had entered to be so talentless. One act was three young girls trying to do a copy version of the Supremes. I have never heard three people so off key in all my days. Talk about the cat's chorus. It was ear-plug time. Billy suggested that they should be renamed 'the Extremes'! One poor bloke thought he was the spitting image of Tom Jones and was even under the misconstrued idea that he sounded like him as well. I would have hated to burst his bubble, but Tom is *not* less than five feet tall, bald, and sounding like he was a poor unfortunate feline being put through a clothes mangle. Not in a month of Sundays!

Seriously though, the worst act turned out to be the last competitor. This was a certain middle-aged stout and formidable lady named Madge 'Ballbreaker' McManus. (She was a female version of Rocky Marciano, but she had more facial hair growth.) May I at this juncture point out something of significance that my Uncle Paddy related to me on more than one occasion? Allow me a few moments while I recall it, as it most surely has great bearing to the following proceedings.

'Be wary, my boy, whom you call talentless,' Uncle Paddy said, and looked so intensely into my eyes that he gave the impression that my very life could depend on his advice. 'Aye, for sure, it is often the case that the most talentless people can sometimes be the most offended.'

Now don't laugh, but Madge's act was *supposed* to be an impersonation of none other than the incomparable Barbra Streisand. Believe you me, Barbra had very little to worry about. Madge's rendition of 'People' (by the way, one of my all-time favourite songs) was absolutely dreadful. It was so bad that all I can compare it to someone being slowly throttled to death. It made the very hairs on the back of your head stand up in fright. It's amazing what effect music can have on one, especially bad music!

Luckily, the ordeal of listening to her was coming to a rapid and a merciful end until Jack Moriarty, another local tough nut who was built like a brick shit-house, stood up and announced, 'Get off the stage, you sour-faced ol' biddy. I have never heard such a flamin' racket in my entire life!'

Now this is where Uncle's Paddy's relevant advice hits home. Don't ask me why, but from the look on Madge's face, I had the definite feeling that she didn't take too kindly to being informed that she didn't quite have the . . . eh . . . X-Factor.

Unsurprisingly, the talent show was soon abandoned after 'Barbra' grabbed hold of a nearby beer bottle and launched it with such amazing accuracy that it struck poor ol' Jack straight between the eyes. What a shot! He went down like a giant oak tree, face first. Madge then made a far from elegant theatrical exit. Manny Goldstein, an elderly Jewish neighbour, remarked as he was passing by at the time that this incident reminded him of the tale of David and Goliath. It's so true. However much you try, there always seems to be an allusion to a Bible story somewhere.

Chapter Eighteen

'Life is can be one helluva of a truly wonderful and amazing place to be, if only people would keep their eyes open to this marvellous fact.' My Aunt Dorothy was in one of her dreamy moods. Yet to be fair to her, she was making a really good and down-to-earth point. With this in mind, take me for instance. I was in the park the other day, eating fish and chips from a newspaper. Now you might not consider this much of story to report, even though the cod was as fresh as a daisy, the chips were chopped up nice and small, and the mushy peas were delicious—delightful! No, the latter is not the illustration I am trying to relate. It was the story in the slightly creased newspaper that I held in my fishy hands.

There it was in black and white, this incredible scoop with the eye-popping headline:

MAN MARRIES HIS DOG!

I swear this is a hundred-per-cent true! It showed this Indian chappie called Arum after the ceremony with his bride. Both were looking blissfully happy. This was very touching, except for the obvious fact that she, the bride, was a dog. Apparently, he led a bit of a sheltered life on a remote farm outside Calcutta and had met Desdemona, a greyhound, completely by accident. She was a stray who just happened to wander into his farmyard one day. It was reported that they hit it off straight away, and after a whirlwind romance, he proposed and she barked three times, which was what he asked her to do to show she was serious. Now listen to me. I am only reporting the facts. Seriously, I am not trying to put the dampers on this affair, and I know I haven't been around that long, but don't you need a license for this type of thing? I should imagine that it would be something more than a dog-license though.

Maybe someone in authority could clear up this sensitive and slightly bizarre matter and set the record straight. Anyway, whatever happens to them, I hope that they both have a very long and a happy future together. I must admit, though, that Desdemona looked quite splendid in her pink chiffon tutu dress. Pink was definitely her colour, as it matched her eyes to perfection.

Life goes on, and it crosses my mind that it has been a fair while since I have visited my Uncle Mike, Ma's elder brother, who lives in a basement flat in Ledbury Road. I must declare that I did find him a wee bit eccentric though. His basement flat resembled a sort of Aladdin's Cave, with papers and magazines and every conceivable object picked up on his travels, including a boomerang and a stuffed koala bear. His habitation was even more 'eclectic' in the evening, when he never switched any electric lights on but used candles instead.

Uncle Mike was very similar to Ma in build. He was constructed like an indestructible battleship, small and very stocky. He had a ruddy, fiercely glowing face. Margaret said this was simply due to all the time he had spent under the scorching sun in the Australian outback, where he worked as an itinerant worker.

He had many a tale to tell me, I can tell you, concerning life under the starry, starry Aussie skies. One such tale was how when he would go to sleep in his tent in the outback at night, he would always place a hammer under his pillow. This was so that if any reptile should have the audacity to crawl into his abode, he would smash the flamin' smithereens out of it.

To be fair, Mike was a hospitable person, but he had the rather annoying habit of not using implements such as knives or forks whilst eating. On such occasions, when he offered me a something to eat, it was usually covered in coal dust, as he had usually just stoked the fire with his bare mitts before doing so. However, I for my part, like an idiot, was too polite to refuse him, and gracefully accepted his offerings but always ended up with a churning stomach upset afterwards.

Grandma says that there is a lot that we have to put up with in life, but we show that we are true Christians when we display tolerance and love. Amen!

Chapter Nineteen

It's amazing what tasty morsels of gossip one can pick up if one can zoom in on some of the many local gossipers. Mrs McHendry and Mrs Phelan were in a right ol' state when the former revealed that she had caught her husband wearing some of her clothes. And the latter astonishingly revealed that her better half was going to the hairdresser's to have his hair done. She was none too impressed though. 'A cross between Sophia Loren and Elizabeth Taylor was the style he was seeking! In a month of Sundays, can you believe it?'

Both ladies were at their wits end what to do. They were debating whether or not to shower both their straying husbands with several gallons of holy water to appease the spirit world and help to set matters straight. It was, for certain and without a shadow of a doubt, another one of those conundrums, never easy to unravel. To top it all, as if they both hadn't enough to put up with already, some 'right ol' stirrers' in the neighbourhood were unforgivably mixing it even further by suggesting that both of the husbands were now looking so much better than their plain-looking wives!

Do you know what? I can't understand why 'Saucy Sandra' doesn't get her window sash fixed. It gave away again the other day, but on this occasion there were two naked people in full view, the two people being Sandra as well as the 'Colonel'. He was strung up like a chicken, and I couldn't say what was happening to him. However, all I could think of at the time was, 'Thank heavens I had already eaten!'—not to mention in the meantime how Sandra managed to cover his manhood with his hat with such agility.

I've never seen her move so fast, as she was no spring chicken herself. Strangely, the Colonel's posh hat somehow defied the law of gravity by staying up without any apparent help! All I am prepared to say is that her story of him being her uncle was as empty as a politician's promise. Funny, but I can never seem to see too much of the Colonel after that. It was a total mystery. Maybe, he was posted . . . umm . . . abroad to keep the Army's end up!

Chapter Twenty

Just when I was thinking life was a peach and I was toying with the orgasmic idea of being a modern-day Casanova, three things jettisoned my hopes. There are no prizes for guessing who jettisoned them! The first incident happened during Mr Harper's history lesson. I was sitting in the left back row concentrating on all the facts, dates, and explanations of why some countries are never happy unless they are kicking the proverbial pants off another poor sod of a country. It's true!

Jennifer was seated in the middle row right opposite myself. Now, there was no feasible explanation for what she did next—not in a hundred million years. She caught my attention by allowing her gaze to wander down her right thigh, as she lifted up her skirt to reveal the outer limits of her floral knickers! I ask you! How in the name of the heavens is a fellow supposed to focus his attention on schoolwork with all this going on? There should be a law. She then started to lick her lips, and I couldn't stop imagining those very lips were licking me all over. It wasn't my fault in the least, and after a few minutes I came to the conclusion that I couldn't care less if Wellington, Napoleon, or the pop group Abba won the battle of Waterloo.

If this wasn't bad enough, a few days later (by which time I must confess I had almost recovered my senses) I was coming down the school corridor and noticed Jennifer coming towards me. Upon noticing me, her eyes lit up like what I can only describe as two small furnaces. Consequently, and without a shadow of a doubt, I felt her eyes like two laser beams transfix me in their intensity. If I had had the will power I most certainly would have fled. Unfortunately, I was a complete goner.

Jennifer proceeded to skilfully steer me into the school janitor's cupboard, which was located on this particular corridor. Eventually, she began to ravage me like some kind of a wild tigress. Honestly, I have always had an odd penchant for wild tigresses and in my humble opinion, each to his own.

Mind you, I must say our lovemaking was a wee bit on the precarious side as we dodged in and out of old blackboards, worn out canes, and three-legged chairs. Putting the case mildly, I was so glad that no teachers happened to come into our love nest. They would have probably had some kind of a coronary. I was on the verge of having one myself.

'I have always desired you, and I must beg you to come to my cousin's party on the King's Road as my date!' She was playing with me like a kitten would play with a reel of cotton, which to be honest is a relatively harmless game.

'Please, stop toying with me Jennifer. I know you have the hots for "Flashman". Please do us both a favour and don't deny it.'

'Oh, him! I have now grown out of flash suits, cars, and penthouses.'

I know this might sound pathetic, but I had always had the feeling she would grow out of her yuppie phase one day.

'Don't know if I can make it anyway. I would have to check my diary.'

'Check it now!'

'Sorry, can't!'

'Why not?'

'It's at home.'

It sounded a good idea at the time. I checked out my diary when I got home, but it will come as no surprise that it was alarmingly empty. I was going to tell her that I was busy as I had a Spanish girlfriend who lived in Barcelona and wrote to me every Saturday night, but after serious consideration I thought I wouldn't bother.

Again, I agreed to turn up to the party with my 'non-girlfriend', knowing full well that it was a lost cause. After I arrived, I soon discovered that 'Jezebel' and 'Flashman' had had a furious row, and I discovered that Jennifer was only using me to get back at him. After their theatrical confrontation and much finger-pointing, both of them stormed out. I don't know, but it was all a bit too much for me. Of course, this left me starkly dateless. Thereupon, accepting my fate, I faced reality like a man and grabbed as much food and drink from the generous host as I could, before deciding to scarper off in order to have an early night.

I walk along the Chelsea Embankment. It is so calm and tranquil, and the world felt like it had settled down to a thankful slumber.

Suddenly, I have an indefinable urge to grow up so that I could spread my wings and fly away. Nevertheless, in the wee, wee hours of this still morning I wondered why we lived in a society which can only be described as 'me, Me, ME!'

It is fascinating but true that I used to know an eastern girl who was called this. I believed she worked at the Chinese takeaway.

Chapter Twenty-One

Back at the Gardens I have made friends with an elderly Indian couple called Mr and Mrs Patel. They are really lovely and friendly people, and I like them very much. I feel I have kind of been of adopted by them, as they don't have any children of their own. Mrs Patel is a brilliant cook, but she is always insisting that I eat more and more of her culinary delights. This lovely ol' dear is forever coercing me to partake of curries, samosas, poppadoms, and Indian ice creams. Now I do admit that she does mean well, and I don't wish to sound like I am not very grateful. However, I cannot but notice that my waistline is gradually getting wider and wider.

They are both stoutly built but very homely, and there is nothing quite like Mrs Patel's welcoming hug. It's a bit like a friendly python. Coincidentally, this leads quite nicely on to the subject of their rather special or—how should I say?—unique pet. Have you guessed what it is yet? No? Well, I did give you a strong hint. It *is* actually a python. It's about six feet long and it is rather exotically named Mango.

I am quite partial to Mango, and I know he likes me, but he does have this rather annoying habit of wrapping himself a bit cosily, may I say, around my groin. Yes, maybe it's just that he is being very friendly. Nonetheless, I do get a bit concerned that he might overdo it somewhat in this rather sensitive area—so much so that vital bits might actually drop right off. Strange things can occur when the blood circulation is curtailed, or so I have been told. It will come as no startling revelation that I have reached the conclusion that Mango is gay. Now don't get me wrong. I have no problem with that. Pythons, like people, have their own sexual orientation, and that's just the way things are. Let nature take its course.

'Life is full of idiosyncrasies, and that's a blessed and holy fact, and that it most certainly is.' Auntie May was in full flow and do you know what?

She was darned right, spot on. Take, for instance, my brother Michael. He has invented a new word. Yes siree, he has. And that new word which might one day be embraced wholeheartedly into the English Language is 'drud'. Don't ask me why he invented it. Maybe he felt in all honesty that there wasn't a term that quite covered 'lazy, slothful, and downright bone-idle', but that about summed up the meaning of his gem.

Rita has a friend called Angie who is a very nice girl but has this rather annoying habit of talking to everyone all kind of posh and disdainful. And what is even more tiresome is that she has this tendency to look down her nose at one whilst doing so. In the circumstances it is kind of amusing since she is hardly descended from the aristocracy, being from our part of town. Very peculiar! I can only hope it is not catching. Rita beware!

Billy and I certainly hit the bullseye the other evening after a somewhat indifferent week when we hit upon a new Irish pub called the Pickled Parrot. What a great name! Appearing at this promising venue was a new and up-and-coming comedian called Kevin Cumlately (his stage name, I believe). It was well known that he was blessed with gift of the Blarney.

> A fellow went into a pub and said to the landlord that he wanted a pint of bitter. After he was served, he proceeded to walk straight up the wall, right across the ceiling, and came down the other side of the wall, before eventually walking straight out of the pub's rear exit. After this, one of the regulars turned to the landlord and proclaimed how absolutely incredible it was what he had just witnessed. The landlord turned to the customer and said it was incredible because yesterday he had ordered a lager!

What an out-of-this-world dream I had the other night! A corker of corkers! Ship ahoy! Full speed ahead! Let me give you the full and unadulterated details. Wow! I can hardly describe all that was happening. I was the only passenger on a luxury liner named the *Erotica*. What a ship! Talk about five-star service. This one was seven-star and rising. And more to the point, what a sensational crew! Q-u-i-n-t-e-s-s-e-n-t-i-a-l!

Aye, for sure, it was equipped with all the usual modern perks such as swimming pools, sun decks, private cinemas, and loads of different restaurants. It goes without saying that I was spoiled for choice. The captain even let me steer the ship. There's nothing much to it really. When

I get older, as well as getting my own boat, I'll get my pilot's license to fly around the world and the big house and gardens, as well as about five hot cars to fill up the driveway. The football pools coupon had better come up trumps, because otherwise all of this could be only a dream. Ah, but what a dream . . .

Getting back to my present fantasy, what was so extraordinary about it and was definitely the highlight (along with the wonderful views as I sailed the seven seas) was that there were five female masseuses on board. Need I say more? Their sole purpose was to look after my every need. I know what you are thinking—that these five gorgeous chicks might have taken advantage of me. Not on your nelly! Everything was above board, ship-shape and proper. And that's my story, and as this is my dream, you will just have to take my word for it—Captain's honour!

Each lovely lass, apart from being a wonderful touch, had a special qualification—reflexology, aromatherapy, Swedish massage, acupuncture, and Reiki to name a few. I'll tell you something else for nothing, and that is there is very little to compare to someone who has a kind and loving touch. It's a gift for sure, bestowed on mankind from above from a loving and beautiful God. And that's my point of view and I am surely sticking to it.

I am not trying to sound sensational or confrontational, but when one of the lovely and delightful maidens gave you the full works, so as to speak, you could, believe you me, feel more than likely that you were actually residing in heaven. It's so very, very true. There is a trick to getting the best from this technique. To put it in a nutshell, surrender to the touch and you'll be there in Nirvana in double-quick time. Scout's honour! Straight up!

However, if you are fortunate enough to have five raving beauties lovingly working on you at a particular moment in time, there are not quite enough words in the English dictionary to put you completely in the picture. Nevertheless, I'll give you two words that might vaguely stir up your imagination and they are 'utter bliss'!

Of course, there is a slight problem with all this excitement. What do you think that could be? Well, the trouble is that every time I have a dream like this, I wake up with the sheets soaking wet. It's not funny! Ma keeps on questioning me as to why the sheets are soiled. She's even suggested that I'm keeping 'girlie magazines' under my pillow and at night having a crafty and shifty look at them every now and again. Charming!

Sadly, the truth is I wouldn't mind looking at them, but I simply can't afford them in the first place anyway. 'Sex-starved and skint' could be my obituary, if I am not too careful.

I have come to the rapid conclusion that I need a holiday. Especially, after the Pickled Parrot has installed a parrot to say—now can you believe it?—'How big is your willy?' Folks are getting very enterprising these days, don't you agree?

It's great once in a while to have a 'happy hour', and I am not talking here about a boozy session, although there is nothing actually wrong with that so long as one doesn't overdo it. No, when I think of a 'happy hour', the one I have in mind is when we take time out to think of all the things that we have to be happy about—absolutely everything you can think of. Never mind if there are only three or four things that leap to mind. It will be just great to focus on these joyful things for at least an hour. I am sure that doing so can lift up the spirit and leave the doldrums behind.

Take it up today and feel the benefits of a radiant and a happy heart! Keep at it! It's worth the effort! I am still manfully plugging away. Practise makes perfect. Phew! I am feeling so much better in myself already. And that joyful and radiant face in the mirror—is that actually me? It can give you a warm glow, but make sure that you are not sitting on the oven whilst doing this or else you might go up in smoke!

Wow! I do feel good, especially as the Council have told my family that we will be rehoused in the near future. What brilliant news! No more coal to be fetched from the coalman. And the thought of having my own bath and shower is enough to make me go into my Gene Kelly mode as I would go splashing about like he did in 'Singin' in the Rain'. Life's a pearl, and I am going to give it my best shot. Bullseye! You had better believe it. The good times are heading my way. And they're here to stay come what may. Okay?

It's going to be the ride of my young life. Right on!

Billy heard a joke the other day. It went something like this.

An Irishman went on holiday in Spain. One of the main intentions of the holiday was to see a bullfight, which he had never seen before. He booked a hotel near the bullring so he wouldn't have far to travel to this event. The day before this spectacle he decided to go out for a meal and have it near the bullfighting arena. He came across a restaurant offering a

'Spanish Special Soup'. He thought it would be a good idea to try a local dish, so he went in and was greeted jovially by the manager, who said that he had made a wise choice, for this meal was a local favourite. Paddy was presented with the dish, which had fairly large balls in it. He ate it and thought it was delicious and came back the next day shortly before the bullfight and ordered the same dish again. He enjoyed it immensely but noticed the balls were very much smaller than they were the day before. He enquired of the manager who explained.

'It is quite simple, Senor. The reason is that on some particular moments the matador wins the fight, but on other occasions, it is sometimes the bull!'

It might seem a funny thing to say, but when I move to another location I will miss this place. Life can be so contradictory as well as being ironic. What is that quaint expression when one tries to attempt to describe something like this? I think it is 'with warts and all'. But how can I completely forget those grimy walls, ceilings, roads, and pavements, not to mention other places—the rubbish-strewn streets and petrol-stained alleyways, the graffiti sprayed on every conceivable object. Not to mention the various sounds of stressed-out voices and high-pitched radios and stereo systems blazing forth from every possible angle. Happy days!

'Take a break! Get away from it all and see the world!' proclaims Matt, my Australian buddy, who is on a worldwide trip. The lucky beggar! I am already counting the days as well as the pennies to get myself in motion. I really admire dudes like Matt who get off their bums and do something with their lives. I also admire people who are a shining light in their own particular and unique way. I am sure you, Dear Reader, know that I cannot sing the praises of my Ma high enough. Rock on, Ma, forever!

'Finally, when all is said and done Ireland should be declared a 'worldwide-safety-heritage-zone!' Uncle Paddy paused to take a large sip from one of his potent home-grown brews. 'I really do. And the sooner the flamin' better, as far as I am concerned, because when it comes to religion and politics, we are in serious danger of kicking the living shite out of each other!'

What is there left to say (apart from everything I can't recall or forgot to mention)? Strategically though, as I ascend up to the roof, I feel the wheels of my brain working. (Worryingly, I think I can literally hear them too in a natural sort of way making the join-ups!) Anyhow, I have recently come to the inventive conclusion that my cool idea of going off to outer space now needs a more modern-day approach. It does. Not in a chariot with two horses who ordinarily wouldn't make it a few feet off the ground. Now be fair, they wouldn't, would they? No, I am thinking of a sort of supersonic space vehicle on Route 66 (celestial mode, of course). I think I'll drop a line to NASA to mention what I have in mind.

There is nothing quite like it. I mean *really* getting away from it all (far from the madding crowd and all that jazz). Phew! I am popping my cork at the mere thought of this fantastic once-in-a-lifetime journey beyond the stars. Therefore, after seeing myself being securely strapped in and observing my own personal star shining in the wide deep yonder, my longing heart will be finally content. Aye, aye, aye, really getting away from it all! Hallelujah! Hallelujah!!

It's such an encouraging and loving thought to have embedded in my heart and soul.

A sort of double-aye, if you get my drift! I am sure you do, don't you?! Of course you do. So there's is nothing really left to say apart from 'May the Good Lord always smile upon you . . .

. . . AND I HOPE—I WILL SEE YOU THHHERRREEEE!!!!!!!!!!!'

Author Biography

Kevin Barry is a fifty-nine year old artist who has had three one-man painting exhibitions in London. This is his second publication. The first was *World Traveller*. The latter was series of short stories from around the world.

The author is an extensive worldwide traveller. He is a great believer in art for everybody, both young and old folk, for self-expression and to sense and feel the joy of life.